Contents

To the Student

The Student Activities Manual to accompany *¡Anda! Curso elemental, Volume 1* is a completely integrated manual that includes "workbook" activities as well as audio activities and others based on the reading and video series *Ambiciones siniestras*. The activities in each chapter mirror the structure and content of the *¡Anda!* textbook and offer extensive practice of the vocabulary and grammar chunks as well as the cultural topics introduced in your text. Preliminary Chapter A provides you the opportunity to build on the initial points presented in the text, while Recycling Chapter 6 offers activities based on a cumulative review. Now you're ready to go!

Special features of the Student Activities Manual include the following:

- Recording activities with which to practice language proficiency and fluency by providing oral responses online
- *Más cultura* activities provide additional cultural information relating to the main themes in the textbook chapters
- Engaging art- and photo-based activities
- *Comunidades* activities (experiential and service learning) that correlate to the main themes of each chapter
- *Heritage Language* activities that encourage all Spanish learners to reflect on the language and its culture. They will also elevate your level of performance.
- Section headings that include the corresponding textbook pages for reference
- Electronic version also available on *MySpanishLab*

Nombre: ______________________ Fecha: ______________________

A-07 Heritage Language: *tu mundo hispano*. As you have learned, customs and word choice in greetings vary within the Spanish-speaking world. If you are of Spanish-speaking heritage, take a moment to consider the customs of your own culture. If you are not, interview a friend, relative or fellow student from your campus who is of Spanish-speaking heritage in order to find out about how people in that specific country greet each other.

Paso 1. Write at least five questions that you will reflect on or that you will ask the person that you plan to interview. The following are some ideas to consider while formulating your questions: gestures used while greeting others, variations in practices based on the gender and age of the person to greet, variations based on type of relationship, generational differences, and cultural variations and differences.

____

____

____

____

____

Paso 2. If you are of Spanish-speaking heritage, reflect on the questions that you have written above and write in Spanish about how your cultural heritage compares to the customs described in your textbook and to the customs in the United States that you have experienced firsthand. If you are not of Spanish-speaking heritage, use the questions from **Paso 1** to guide you through an interview of a Hispanic friend, relative or fellow student from your campus. Then write in English about how that person's practices compare to the customs described in your textbook and to your own customs.

____

____

____

____

____

Nombre: Matthew Worns Fecha: W2

Vocabulario

2. Expresiones útiles para la clase (Textbook p. 8)

A-08 ¿Qué significa? One of your friends from Spanish class is having difficulty understanding some of the new vocabulary that you are learning. Answer each of her questions in English.

MODELO ¿Qué significa "escriba"?
Write

1. ¿Qué significa "vayan a la pizarra"? Go to the board.
2. ¿Qué significa "lea el libro"? read your. book
3. ¿Qué significa "escuchen"? listen.
4. ¿Qué significa "conteste, por favor"? Answer,. please
5. ¿Qué significa "abran el libro"? Close your. book
6. ¿Qué significa "escriba en la pizarra"? Write on your board

A-09 ¿Cómo se dice en español? Your classmate is having difficulty remembering how to say some of the new vocabulary. Use the following expressions to answer his questions. Give your responses orally.

No comprendo.	¿Qué significa?	De nada.	¿Qué es esto?
No lo sé.	Repita, por favor.	¿Quién?	

1. ¿Cómo se dice "I don't know" en español? No lo sé
2. ¿Cómo se dice "repeat, please" en español? Repita, por favor
3. ¿Cómo se dice "what is this" en español? ¿Que es esto?
4. ¿Cómo se dice "I don't understand" en español? No comprendo
5. ¿Cómo se dice "what does it mean" en español? ¿Que significa?
6. ¿Cómo se dice "who" en español? ¿Quien?
7. ¿Cómo se dice "you're welcome" en español? De nada

Nombre: ______________________________ Fecha: ______________________

A-16 Heritage Language: *tu español.* In Spanish, because some letters have the same sound associated with them, there are words that are commonly misspelled. For example, **b** and **v** are easily confused, as are **ll** and **y, g** and **j** and also, particularly in the case of people from Latin America, **c, s** and **z.** It can also be especially difficult to remember when to use the silent **h.** Help yourself become more aware of and avoid making common spelling mistakes. For each word you hear, write the correct spelling.

1. ______________________________.
2. ______________________________.
3. ______________________________.
4. ______________________________.
5. ______________________________.
6. ______________________________.
7. ______________________________.
8. ______________________________.

Vocabulario

4. Los cognados (Textbook p. 10)

A-17 Categorías. As you know, many words in Spanish are very similar to words in English that have the same meaning. Demonstrate your understanding of the cognates below by correctly placing each word in its most appropriate category.

1. el hospital	people	places	foods
2. el actor	people	places	foods
3. el tomate	people	places	foods
4. el director	people	places	foods
5. el restaurante	people	places	foods
6. el novelista	people	places	foods
7. el mango	people	places	foods
8. el bar	people	places	foods
9. el aeropuerto	people	places	foods
10. el chocolate	people	places	foods
11. el artista	people	places	foods
12. la pizza	people	places	foods

Nombre: ______________________________ Fecha: ______________________

A-18 Comparación y contraste. Use your understanding of cognates to identify the meaning of the following words and then match each word to its most logical opposite.

1. similar _____ a. horrible
2. optimista _____ b. pesimista
3. importante _____ c. diferente
4. fantástico _____ d. trivial
5. especial _____ e. tragedia
6. comedia _____ f. normal

A-19 ¿Cómo se pronuncia? Although cognates are spelled similarly in Spanish and English, they often sound very different. Listen to the native Spanish speaker pronounce the following words. Then give your personal best Spanish pronunciation of each word.

1. conclusión
2. responsabilidad
3. idea
4. televisión
5. imposible
6. universidad
7. generoso
8. ideal
9. biotecnología
10. dólar

Nombre: ______________________ Fecha: ______________________

Gramática

5. Los pronombres personales (Textbook p. 11)

A-20 Los pronombres. Fill in each blank with the correct subject pronoun in Spanish.

MODELO I
yo

1. you (singular, formal) ________________.
2. they (a group of men) ________________.
4. you (plural; a group of women, informal, in Spain) ________________.
5. we (two men) ________________.
6. we (a group of women) ________________.
7. you (plural; in Latin America) ________________.
8. you (singular, informal) ________________.

A-21 Los amigos. Your new friend Laura from Argentina has invited you to a party at her apartment so that you can get to know some of her other friends. Fill in the blanks with the subject pronouns she needs to use to talk about herself and her friends.

MODELO my friends watching TV in the living room (all men)
ellos

1. The men that are playing pool ________________.
2. My sister and I ________________.
3. My girlfriends over there on the other side of the room ________________.
4. My brother ________________.
5. You (singular, informal) ________________.
6. My boyfriend and I ________________.
7. My friends over there dancing (both men and women) ________________.
8. You and your best friend ________________.

Nombre: ______________________________ Fecha: ______________________

Nota cultural: ¿Tú o usted? (Textbook p. 12)

A-22 ¿Tú o usted? Based on what you have learned about how the use of **tú** and **usted** has evolved over time, choose the phrase that best completes each of the following statements. More than one may be correct.

1. In general, I should use the **tú** form when I am talking with…

   ______ people that I know well.

   ______ people whose names I do not know.

   ______ members of my family.

   ______ people older than I.

2. If I go to a supermarket in a Spanish-speaking country,

   ______ I must address the clerk as **tú.**

   ______ it is now generally acceptable to address the clerk as **tú.**

   ______ the clerk will be offended if I address him as **tú.**

   ______ it would be fine to address the clerk as **usted.**

3. If I am talking to young people in Latin America,

   ______ they will probably address me as **tú.**

   ______ they will probably address me as **usted.**

   ______ they will probably address me as **vosotros.**

   ______ they might address me as **vos.**

4. I can use the **usted** form in order to…

   ______ show someone that I think they are really old.

   ______ show someone respect.

   ______ play it safe in an uncertain situation.

   ______ show people that I want to be on a first-name basis with them.

5. In Spain, the **vosotras** form is used…

   ______ to talk to more than one female person, or "you all."

   ______ to talk to men and women in an informal setting.

   ______ to talk to more than one male person, or "you all."

   ______ to talk to people in any setting.

6. In Argentina, Costa Rica and other parts of Latin America, **vos…**

   ______ is sometimes used in place of **usted.**

   ______ is sometimes used in place of **vosotros.**

   ______ is sometimes used in informal situations.

   ______ is sometimes used in place of **tú.**

Nombre: ______________________________ Fecha: ______________________

A-23 ¿Cómo hablo con las diferentes personas? You are studying abroad in Spain and come into contact with a variety of people on a daily basis. For the people below, indicate which subject pronouns (**tú, usted, vosotros,** or **ustedes**) you will use when you first meet with them.

1. The mother and father in your host family ______________.
2. The children in your host family ______________.
3. The young program assistant that works with new students during the orientation program ______________.
4. The older man at the kiosk where you buy your newspaper every morning ______________.
5. Your classmates at the university ______________.
6. The server at the corner café where you stop every morning to have a cup of coffee ______________.

A-24 ¿Relación formal o informal? Listen to the following conversations and then select the type of relationship the people have. Select **no se sabe** if the relationship is not known from the context.

1. informal formal no se sabe
2. informal formal no se sabe
3. informal formal no se sabe
4. informal formal no se sabe
5. informal formal no se sabe

Nombre: ______________________ Fecha: ______________________

A-25 Heritage Language: *tu español*. As you have learned, the use of formal and informal pronouns varies across the Spanish-speaking world. If you are of Hispanic heritage, consider your own cultural practices. If you are not, contact a Spanish-speaking friend, relative, or fellow student and ask the person about how people in that person's specific country of origin address each other.

Paso 1. Use the following questions as a guide for your reflection about your own cultural heritage or for your interview and write brief responses for each question.

1. When you speak to your parents or your grandparents do you use **tú** or **usted**? How do you think they would react if you were to use the other term?

   ____.

2. When you speak to close friends do you use **tú** or **usted**? How do you think they would react if you were to use the other term?

   ____.

3. In academic and professional settings, when do people in your country use **tú** and when do they use **usted**?

   ____.

4. When you address someone as **usted** does the other person usually respond to you using **usted** as well? Why or why not?

   ____.

5. Do you ever use **vos** or **vosotros**? In what situations and with whom?

   ____.

6. According to your knowledge and experience, do the customs you have described reflect the customs of most people in your country? How about the customs of other Spanish-speaking countries?

   ____.

Paso 2. A common mistake made by many students of Spanish and also by heritage speakers of Spanish is the use of both **tú** and **usted** in the same sentence with the same person, or the use of the inappropriate register in a specific context. In order to avoid making these mistakes, write appropriate expressions for each of the following people:

- **Abuela (*Grandmother*)**

7. Saludo: ____.
8. Despedida: ____.

- **Mejor amigo/a (*Best friend*)**

9. Saludo: ____.
10. Despedida: ____.

- **Jefe en el trabajo (*boss at work*)**

11. Saludo: ______________________.

12. Despedida: ______________________.

- **Profesor/a**

13. Saludo: ______________________.

14. Despedida: ______________________.

- **Compañero de clase**

15. Saludo: ______________________.

16. Despedida: ______________________.

- **Dependiente de una tienda (*sales associate at a store*)**

17. Saludo: ______________________.

18. Despedida: ______________________.

- **Cliente de tu negocio (*a customer or client of your own business*)**

19. Saludo: ______________________.

20. Despedida: ______________________.

Paso 3. Take a moment to consider the information that you collected in **Paso 1** and how you applied your knowledge in **Paso 2** in order to write a brief reflection in English on how this information has reinforced and/or modified your understanding of formal versus informal address in Spanish and how it compares to English. What are some strategies that you can use to demonstrate feelings like respect or personal closeness when speaking English? Is it possible to use these in Spanish as well? Why or why not? What are some strategies in Spanish that are not available in English? Have you discovered anything interesting about how specific practices vary across different Hispanic cultures?

21. ______________________

____

____

____

Gramática

6. El verbo *ser* (Textbook p. 13)

A-26 ¿Quién es? A friend from your class is having difficulty figuring out to whom the following sentences refer because he does not realize that in Spanish, subject pronouns are not necessary to communicate the subject of a verb. Help him by looking at each form of the verb **ser** and then writing the appropriate subject pronoun(s) in the space provided.

1. ____________________ soy romántico.
2. ____________________ somos profesores.
3. ____________________ eres importante.
4. ____________________ sois generosos.
5. ____________________ son idealistas.
6. ____________________ es ecologista.

A-27 ¿Cómo es tu personalidad? For each of the adjectives below, indicate if they apply to your personality by writing **soy** or **no soy** in the space provided.

1. ____________________ inteligente.
2. ____________________ idealista.
3. ____________________optimista.
4. ____________________ ecologista.
5. ____________________ diferente.
6. ____________________ activista.
7. ____________________ pesimista.

A-28 ¿Cómo son? Complete the sentences with the correct forms of the verb **ser.**

1. Nosotros ____________________ interesantes.
2. La profesora ____________________ idealista.
3. El profesor y usted ____________________ creativos.
4. Los estudiantes y tú ____________________ inteligentes.
5. La profesora y el profesor ____________________ amigos.
6. La clase y yo ____________________ generosos.
7. Tú ____________________ importante.
8. Yo ____________________ realista.

Nombre: ______________________ Fecha: ______________________

A-29 Marta y Gabriela. Listen to Marta describe how she and her sister Gabriela are similar and different, paying special attention to the forms of the verb **ser** that she uses throughout her description. Then, for each adjective, decide whether it applies to **Marta,** to **Gabriela** or to both **Marta y Gabriela** and select the correct name(s).

1. inteligente Marta Gabriela Marta y Gabriela
2. idealista Marta Gabriela Marta y Gabriela
3. realista Marta Gabriela Marta y Gabriela
4. optimista Marta Gabriela Marta y Gabriela
5. creativa Marta Gabriela Marta y Gabriela
6. generosa Marta Gabriela Marta y Gabriela
7. analítica Marta Gabriela Marta y Gabriela

A-30 ¿Cómo son? Describe the people below by using the different components provided to create sentences. Be sure to use the correct forms of **ser.**

MODELO Ella / artista.
Ella es artista. / Es artista.

1. Ellos / diferentes
2. Tú / optimista
3. Yo / inteligente
4. Usted / especial
5. Ella / generosa
6. Nosotros / idealistas
7. Ellos / similares
8. Ellas / activistas
9. Yo / importante
10. Él / novelista

A-31 Heritage Language: *tu español*. In some parts of Latin America many people use the pronoun **vos** in lieu of **tú.** In Spain **vosotros** and **vosotras** are the pronouns used to refer to *you* plural in informal settings. The conjugation of the verb **ser** for **vos** is **sos,** and the conjugation for **vosotros** is **sois.** Listen to each sentence and then indicate which form each speaker uses.

1. vos vosotros / vosotras
2. vos vosotros / vosotras
3. vos vosotros / vosotras
4. vos vosotros / vosotras
5. vos vosotros / vosotras

Vocabulario

7. Los adjetivos de nacionalidad (Textbook p. 14)

A-32 ¿De dónde son? Match the following famous people with their appropriate adjective of nationality.

1. Salma Hayek G	a. es español.
2. Jacques Cousteau C	b. son inglesas.
3. Fidel y Raúl Castro E	c. es francés.
4. Kate y Pippa Middleton B	d. es alemana.
5. Jackie Chan F	e. son cubanos.
6. Claudia Schiffer D	f. es chino.
7. Antonio Banderas A	g. es mexicana.

A-33 Los amigos internacionales. Listen as Susana tells you about her friends from around the world. For each of the people listed below, write down their nationality. Pay special attention to the gender of each friend, and be careful to write the correct form of the verb **ser** and the appropriate masculine or feminine form of the adjectives.

MODELO Carmen *es mexicana.*

1. Kiroko ______________.
2. Antonio y Sara ______________.
3. Olivier ______________.
4. Richard ______________.
5. Ming y Fong ______________.
6. Eulogia ______________.
7. Morenike ______________.
8. Marie ______________.

Nombre: ______________________________ Fecha: ______________________

A-34 Heritage Language: *tu español*. Respond to the following questions.

1. What are your family's countries (or what is your family's country) of origin?

   ____.

2. Conduct research to discover how to say names for those countries (or that country) in Spanish.

   ____.

3. Conduct research to discover the Spanish adjectives to describe people from those countries (or that country). Is the masculine form different from the feminine form for any of the countries? If so, how?

   ____.

Nombre: ______________________ Fecha: ______________________

Nota cultural: Los hispanos (Textbook p. 16)

A-35 Heritage Language: *tu mundo hispano.*

Paso 1. Respond in English to the following questions about cultural identity using the information in your textbook where applicable and your own imagination where necessary.

1. What is the difference between the terms *Hispanic* and *Latino*?

____

____

2. What are some equivalent terms that you could use to describe people from more than one English-speaking country?

____

____

3. If you had to invent a term to refer to all English-speaking people and cultures, what term would you create?

____

____

4. Why do you think many people might prefer to describe themselves using specific adjectives of national identity (**mexicana, colombiano, peruana, argentino**, etc.) instead of using words like *Hispanic* or *Latino*?

____

____

5. Why might some people in some contexts prefer to use the general terms *Hispanic* or *Latino*?

____

____

Paso 2. Interview at least three people of Spanish-speaking heritage in order to find out how they feel about terms like *Hispanic* and *Latino*. Ask them whether or not they like to use these terms when talking about themselves and their families, and how it makes them feel when others use these terms. Write a brief description in English of the results of your interviews and how they have impacted your own understanding of the meaning of these words and how they relate to Hispanic cultures.

____

____

____

____

____

Nombre: ______________________________ Fecha: ______________________

A-46 ¿Qué día?

Paso 1. Look at each sequence of days, find the pattern and select the day that is out of place.

MODELO jueves, martes, sábado, domingo
jueves

1. lunes, martes, viernes, jueves
2. viernes, sábado, domingo, martes
3. domingo, lunes, sábado, miércoles
4. jueves, domingo, lunes, martes
5. miércoles, domingo, viernes, sábado
6. jueves, lunes, sábado, domingo

Paso 2. Now write the day that should take the place of each one you selected in **Paso 1.**

MODELO jueves, martes, sábado, domingo
viernes

7. ____________________.
8. ____________________.
9. ____________________.
10. ____________________.
11. ____________________.
12. ____________________.

A-47 Los días de la semana. Complete the crossword puzzle with the correct days of the week.

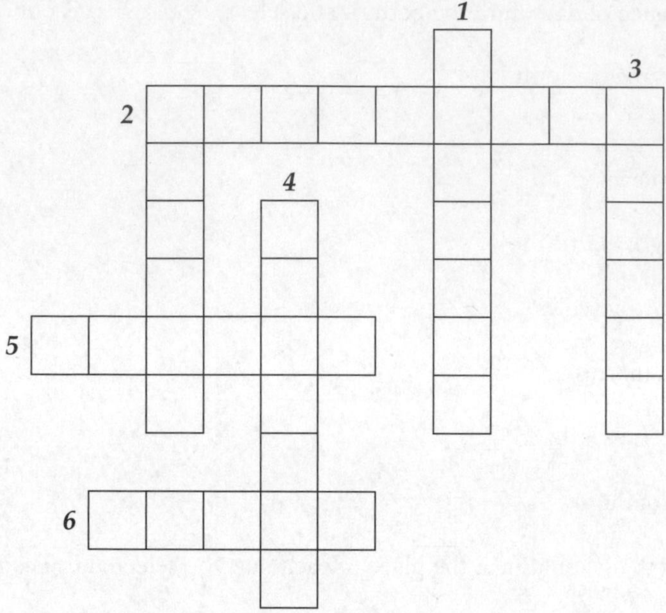

Vertical	**Horizontal**
1. El día antes del (*before*) lunes	2. Dos días antes del viernes
2. Dos días antes del jueves	5. Un día después del (*after*) miércoles
3. Cuatro días antes del miércoles	6. Cuatro días después del jueves
4. El día antes del sábado	

A-48 Los meses. Find the pattern in each sequence, and then fill in each blank with the missing month. Be careful, some of the sequences skip a month or two.

1. diciembre, ____________________, febrero
2. junio, julio, ____________________.
3. ____________________, noviembre, diciembre
4. enero, febrero, ____________________.
5. ____________________, mayo, junio
6. enero, ____________________, mayo, julio
7. abril, ____________________, agosto, octubre
8. abril, julio, ____________________, enero

Nombre: ______________________________ Fecha: ______________________________

A-49 Los meses y los días importantes. Complete the crossword puzzle with the month in which each important day takes place, either in the United States or in the specified country.

Horizontal

1. El día de los veteranos
5. El día de Martin Luther King Jr.
6. El día de San Patricio
7. El día de las madres en los Estados Unidos
8. El día de la Independencia de Los Estados Uniidos
9. El día de San Valentín

Vertical

2. El día Cristóbal Colón (*Columbus*)
3. El día de los presidentes
4. El día de las elecciones

Nombre: ______________________________ Fecha: ______________________

A-50 Heritage Language: *tu mundo hispano*. If you are of Spanish-speaking heritage, describe in Spanish some of the most important holidays in your country or countries of origin, on what days and months you celebrate them, how people generally celebrate them in those countries and how you and your family celebrate them where you live now. How do they compare to important holidays in the United States? If you are not of Spanish-speaking heritage, interview a friend, relative or fellow student from your campus who knows about important holidays in his country of origin. Then list in Spanish each holiday and on what days and months he celebrates them. Finally, in English, describe how people celebrate those holidays and how they compare to holidays that are important to you and your family.

____

____

____

____

____

A-51 Los meses y las estaciones. For each month, write the season of the year that is generally associated with it.

1. septiembre ____________________.
2. julio ____________________.
3. febrero ____________________.
4. octubre ____________________.
5. mayo ____________________.
6. enero ____________________.
7. agosto ____________________.

Nombre: ______________________ Fecha: ______________________

Vocabulario

11. El tiempo (Textbook p. 23)

A-52 El tiempo en el mundo hispano. Listen to the meteorologist's report for the different capitals of Central America, and complete each sentence below using one of the expressions from the word bank. Although more than one option may be valid, you need only choose one for each response.

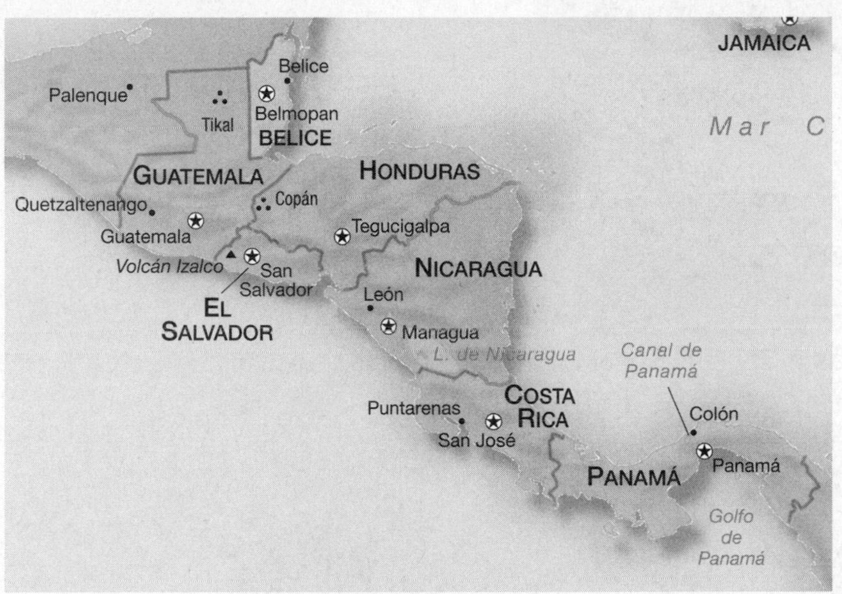

Hace sol.	Hace calor.	Está nublado.	Llueve.	Hace viento.
No hace frío.	No hace calor.	Hace buen tiempo.	Hace mal tiempo.	

1. En San Salvador (El Salvador) ______________________
2. En Guatemala (Guatemala) ______________________
3. En Tegucigalpa (Honduras) ______________________
4. En Managua (Nicaragua) ______________________
5. En San José (Costa Rica) ______________________
6. En Panamá (Panamá) ______________________

Nombre: ______________________ Fecha: ______________________

A-53 ¿Qué tiempo hace? Describe the weather conditions that are depicted in each image, using complete sentences.

MODELO

Está nublado.

1. ______________________

2. ______________________

3. ______________________

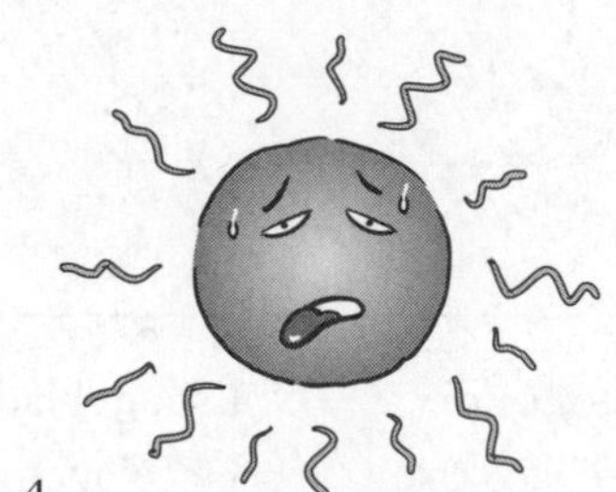

4. ______________________

5. ______________________

Nombre: ______________________ Fecha: ______________________

A-54 ¿Qué tiempo hace en tu zona? For each month below, describe what a typical day would be like in the area where you live.

MODELO octubre
Hace viento y sol.

1. enero ______________________.

2. marzo ______________________.

3. mayo ______________________.

4. julio ______________________.

5. septiembre ______________________.

6. noviembre ______________________.

A-55 Heritage Language: *tú español*. It can be difficult to remember when to use the expression **hace** for some weather expressions and when to use other expressions like **está** in its place. In order to help you remember, for each expression select if it requires **hace, está,** or **nada** (*nothing at all*).

1. llueve
   a. hace
   b. está
   c. nada

2. frío
   a. hace
   b. está
   c. nada

3. viento
   a. hace
   b. está
   c. nada

4. nieva
   a. hace
   b. está
   c. nada

5. sol
   a. hace
   b. está
   c. nada

6. nublado
   a. hace
   b. está
   c. nada

7. calor
   a. hace
   b. está
   c. nada

8. buen tiempo
   a. hace
   b. está
   c. nada

A-56 Las estaciones y el tiempo

Paso 1. Lola is from Cuba and is studying at a university in New England. She has come to realize that the perception of seasons can be very subjective. Look at the table in which she shares her view of the seasons in Cuba and New England, and then answer the questions below.

	Cuba	Nueva Inglaterra
Primavera	febrero, marzo, abril y mayo	abril, mayo, junio
Verano	junio, julio, agosto, y septiembre	julio, agosto
Otoño	octubre, noviembre	septiembre, octubre
Invierno	diciembre, enero	noviembre, diciembre, enero, febrero, marzo

1. Have you ever been to the Caribbean or to New England? If you are not familiar with the weather in those regions, look up the average temperatures for each month of the year. Indicate whether or not you agree with Lola's description of the seasons in those areas and briefly explain why.

2. Give your own subjective description of the seasons in the region where you live. For each season, indicate (in Spanish) which months you associate with it and use the weather expressions you have learned to describe what kind of weather you associate with it.

3. Now choose a city in Argentina, Chile, or Uruguay and look up its average temperatures for each month of the year. For each season, indicate (in Spanish) which months correspond to it in the city you have chosen and use the weather expressions you have learned to describe what kind of weather one may typically encounter at that time of year.

Paso 2. If you are of Spanish-speaking heritage, describe in Spanish the weather and the seasons in your family's country or countries of origin. How do they compare to the place where you now live? How difficult was it for your family to adjust to the climate of the place where you now live? If you are not of Spanish-speaking heritage, interview a friend, relative or fellow student from your campus who is, and describe in Spanish the weather and the seasons in that person's country or countries of origin. Then relate in English how it compares to where the person lives now and how difficult or easy it was for the person's family to adjust to the new climate.

Nombre: ______________________ Fecha: ______________________

Gramática

12. Gustar (Textbook p. 25)

A-57 ¿Qué te gusta? Answer the following questions about your likes and dislikes in complete sentences. Be sure to follow the model closely.

MODELO ¿Te gusta la clase de español?
Sí, me gusta la clase de español. / No, no me gusta la clase de español.

1. ¿Te gustan los lunes?

   ____.

2. ¿Te gustan los viernes?

   ____.

3. ¿Te gusta la música hip-hop?

   ____.

4. ¿Te gusta la música rock?

   ____.

5. ¿Te gusta la nieve?

   ____.

6. ¿Te gusta el viento?

   ____.

7. ¿Te gusta la cafetería de la universidad?

   ____.

A-58 ¿Te gusta? Listen to Ramón's questions about your likes and dislikes and then write your answers below. Be sure to follow the sentence structure in the model closely.

MODELO ¿Te gusta el invierno?
Sí, me gusta el invierno. / No, no me gusta el inverno.

1. ____.
2. ____.
3. ____.
4. ____.
5. ____.
6. ____.

A-59 ¿Y tú? Choose at least five things that you like and record yourself asking a classmate in Spanish if he or she likes them. Remember that each question should begin with "**¿Te gusta...?**" or "**¿Te gustan...?**", depending on whether the things you mention are in the singular or the plural.

Comunidades

A-60 Experiential Learning: *En un restaurante hispano*. Go with a friend to a local Hispanic restaurant and practice greeting the employees and introducing yourselves to them in Spanish. After you leave, make a list of all of the different ways you heard native speakers greet each other and/or introduce each other.

A-61 Service learning: *Profesores particulares*. Contact your university's tutoring center and offer to provide free tutoring services for international students of Spanish-speaking heritage who need help with their English. You may also contact a local community adult education center or church and offer tutoring services in English for adults whose native or heritage language is Spanish. Write a brief letter of introduction, proposing your idea and outlining what specific traits, skills, and knowledge you could contribute and why you feel it is important to use your skills to help others.

Nombre: ______________________ Fecha: ______________________

¿Quiénes somos?

Comunicación I

Vocabulario

1. La familia: Describing families (Textbook p. 32)

01-01 Las familias famosas. Complete the following sentences about famous Hispanic families with the correct vocabulary word.

hijo	padrastro	padres
hija	esposa	madre

1. Antonio Banderas no es el padre de de Dakota y Alexander Johnson-Griffith. Banderas está casado (*is married*) con la madre de ellos (*their mother*), Melanie Griffith. Antonio Banderas es el ______________ de Dakota y Alexander.
2. Melanie Griffith es la ______________ de Antonio Banderas.
3. Antonio Banderas y Melanie Griffith tienen una hija, Stella Banderas Griffith. Ellos son sus ______________.
4. Julio Iglesias es el padre de Enrique Iglesias. Enrique es su ______________.
5. Gloria Estefan tiene dos hijos: Nayib y Emily Estefan; ella es su ______________.
6. El padre de Paloma Picasso Gilot es el famoso pintor, Pablo Picasso. Ella es su ______________.

01-02 Las familias hispanas. Listen to the information about some other famous Hispanic families and then complete the sentences with the correct expressions from the word bank.

La madre	La familia	Los abuelos maternos	Los hermanos
El padre	Los padres	Los abuelos paternos	

1. ____________________ de Cristina Aguilera es estadounidense.
2. ____________________ de Cameron Díaz son cubanos.
3. ____________________ de Salma Hayek son mexicanos.
4. ____________________ de Benicio del Toro es puertorriqueña.
5. ____________________ de Gael García Bernal son mexicanos.
6. ____________________ de Chucho Valdés es cubano.

Nombre: ______________________ Fecha: ______________________

01-03 La familia de Eduardo. Look at Eduardo's family tree and then answer the questions in complete sentences, using the first names of the appropriate family members. Be sure to follow the sentence structure of the model closely and to omit the known subject to avoid being repetitive.

MODELO ¿Quién es el esposo de Francisca?
Es Enrique.

1. ¿Quién es la prima de Sonia? ______________________.
2. ¿Quién es la hermana de Enrique? ______________________.
3. ¿Quién es el hijo de Carmen? ______________________.
4. ¿Quién es la esposa de Enrique? ______________________.
5. ¿Quién es la prima de Antonio? ______________________.
6. ¿Quién es el abuelo de Adriana? ______________________
7. ¿Quién es la tía de Sonia? ______________________.
8. ¿Quién es la madre de Rosario? ______________________.

Nombre: ______________________________ Fecha: ______________________

01-04 Crucigrama. Complete the crossword puzzle with the term that describes each family relationship.

1. La nueva esposa de mi padre es mi (*my*)…
2. La hermana de mi padre es mi…
3. La hija de mis tíos es mi…
4. El hermano de mi madre y la esposa del hermano de mi madre son mis…
5. El padre de mi hermana es mi…
6. La hija de mis padres es mi…
7. La madre de mi madre es mi…
8. El padre de mi madre es mi…
9. Soy el hijo de mi… (*feminine*)
10. El nuevo esposo de mi madre es mi…

Nombre: ______________________ Fecha: ______________________

01-05 Heritage Language: *tu español.* As in every language, both formal and informal expressions exist to refer to family members. If you are of Spanish-speaking heritage, use the words that are part of your own family's customs to answer the following questions. If you are not, then interview a friend, relative or fellow student of Spanish-speaking heritage in order to find out about their practices.

1. When you speak to your mother and your father, what words do you use to address them?

____

2. When your parents speak to you and your siblings, do they always call you by your names? If not, what other terms of endearment do they use?

____

3. What words do you use to refer to your grandparents?

____

4. Does your family use any nicknames or terms of endearment to refer to other family members (aunts and uncles, siblings, cousins)? If so, what are they?

____

Pronunciación: Vowels (Textbook p. 33)

The vowels are nearly always pronounced the same way. Their pronunciation is crisp and shorter than in English. For example:

a like the "a" in *father* but shorter

e like the "e" in *hey* but shorter

i like the "ee" in *meet* but shorter

o like the "o" in *zone* but shorter

u like the "u" in *rule* but shorter

Nombre: ______________________________ Fecha: ______________________

01-06 Palabras incompletas. Listen to each word and fill in the missing vowels.

1. p____dr____str____
2. h____rm____n____
3. ____sp____s____
4. ____b____ ____l____
5. tr____b____j____d____r____
6. ____b____rr____d____
7. r____sp____ns____bl____
8. p____r____z____s____

01-07 Algunos hispanos famosos. Listen to and compare the pronunciation of the following names by the native speaker of Spanish and the native speaker of English. Then give your best imitation of the Spanish speaker's pronunciation, paying special attention to how you pronounce both the sound and the brevity of the vowels.

1. Antonio Banderas
2. Salma Hayek
3. Shakira Mebarak
4. Penélope Cruz
5. Juanes Aristizábal Vásquez
6. Javier Bardem
7. Gael García Bernal
8. Benicio del Toro
9. Alejandro Amenábar
10. Icíar Bollaín

Nombre: ______________________ Fecha: ______________________

01-08 ¿Hablante nativo o no? Listen carefully to the vowels as you hear each word pronounced and then indicate whether or not the person speaking is a native speaker of Spanish by selecting **sí** or **no** for each word.

1. sí no
2. sí no
3. sí no
4. sí no
5. sí no
6. sí no

Nota cultural: Los nombres en el mundo hispano (Textbook p. 33)

01-09 Los matrimonios. Based on what you have learned in this chapter about how women's last names change after marriage in many Hispanic countries, rewrite each woman's full name so that it clearly reflects her marital status.

1. Gloria Fajardo + Emilio Estefan ______________________.
2. Marivi Lorido + Andy García ______________________.
3. Lymari Nadal + Edward James Olmos ______________________.
4. Talisa Soto + Benjamin Bratt ______________________.
5. Janet Templeton + Ramón Estévez ______________________.

01-10 Los apellidos. In **Capítulo 1,** you learned about the ways in which Hispanic last names are passed from parents to children. Complete the following hypothetical sentences with the names as they would be written.

1. If Andy García's daughter had a baby with Gael García Bernal, and they named her Gracia, then her full name would be ______________________.
2. If Gloria and Emilio Estefan's daughter had a son with Emilio Estévez and they named him Esteban, his full name would be ______________________.
3. If Guillermo del Toro's daughter and Benicio del Toro's son had a son and named him Teodoro, his full name would be ______________________.
4. If Penélope Cruz and Tom Cruise had remained together and had a baby, naming him Cruz, then his full name would have been ______________________.
5. If Cameron Díaz and Alex Bueno had a daughter and named her Lola, her full name would be

______________________.

01-11 Nombres curiosos. Listen as the speaker says each name and then give your own best pronunciation, paying special attention to the vowel sounds.

1. …
2. …
3. …
4. …
5. …

Gramática

2. El verbo *tener*: Expressing what someone has (Textbook p. 34)

01-12 ¿Quién tiene? Listen to each sentence, paying special attention to the form of the verb **tener** that you hear. Based on that, select the person or people that could be the subject of each sentence.

1. yo	tú	él	nosotros	ustedes
2. ella	tú	yo	usted	ellos
3. ustedes	yo	ella	nosotros	tú
4. usted	ellas	nosotros	yo	él
5. yo	usted	tú	nosotros	ellos
6. tú	ustedes	nosotros	ella	yo
7. él	nosotros	tú	yo	usted

Nombre: ______________________________ Fecha: ______________________

01-13 La familia de Yolanda. Read the following description of Yolanda's family and then answer the questions according to the information in the passage. Be careful to use the correct form of the verb **tener** in your answers, and follow the model closely.

¡Mi familia es muy grande! Tengo diez hermanos —cuatro hermanas y seis hermanos—. Mi madre también (*also*) tiene cinco hermanos y todos (*all*) ellos tienen esposa. Mi padre es de una familia pequeña, solamente (*only*) tiene una hermana. Ella tiene esposo. En total tengo quince primos; catorce son de la familia de mi madre y uno es el hijo de la hermana de mi padre. En contraste con mi familia, mi esposo Fernando tiene tres hermanos; solamente tiene un tío y una tía, y dos primos.

1. ¿Cuántas hijas tienen los padres de Yolanda?

   a. 3 b. 5 c. 6 d. 7

2. ¿Cuántos hermanos tiene la madre de Yolanda?

   a. 3 b. 5 c. 6 d. 7

3. ¿Cuántos tíos tiene Yolanda?

   a. 4 b. 6 c. 8 d. 10

4. ¿Cuántos nietos tienen los abuelos maternos de Yolanda?

   a. 5 b. 10 c. 12 d. 15

5. ¿Cuántos hijos tienen los padres de Fernando?

   a. 1 b. 2 c. 4 d. 5

6. ¿Cuántos tíos tiene Fernando?

   a. 1 b. 2 c. 3 d. 4

7. ¿Cuántos hijos tienen los tíos de Fernando?

   a. 1 b. 2 c. 3 d. 4

01-14 La familia de Ernesto. Listen as Ernesto describes his family and then select the names that belong in each category.

1. Abuelos maternos:

    _____ Manuel _____ Nerea _____ Francisco _____ Carmen

2. Abuelos paternos:

    _____ Manuel _____ Nerea _____ Francisco _____ Carmen

3. Padres:

    _____ Nerea _____ Francisco _____ Alfonso _____ Pedro _____ María

4. Hermanos:

    _____ Ana _____ Emilia _____ Rubén _____ Justino

    _____ Pedro _____ Clara _____ Antonio

5. Esposos de los hermanos:

    _____ Justino _____ Clemente _____ Ana _____ Pedro _____ Emilia _____ Antonio

6. Hijos de los hermanos:

    _____ Rubén _____ Justino _____ Margarita _____ Ana _____ Antonio _____ Mario

01-15 ¿Y tu familia? Answer the following questions about your own family using complete sentences in Spanish. Be careful to use the correct forms of the verb **tener** in your answers.

MODELO ¿Cuántos abuelos tienes?
Tengo cuatro abuelos. / No tengo abuelos.

1. ¿Cuántos padres tienes? ______________________________
2. ¿Tienes padrastro? ______________________________
3. ¿Cuántos hermanos tienen tus (*your*) padres? ______________________________

    ____
4. ¿Cuántos hermanos tienes? ______________________________
5. ¿Cuántos tíos tienen tus hermanos y tú? ______________________________

    ____
6. ¿Tienen tus hermanos y tú muchos primos? ______________________________

    ____
7. ¿Cuántos abuelos tienen tus hermanos y tú? ______________________________

    ____

Nombre: ______________________ Fecha: ______________________

01-16 Heritage Language: *tu español.* As you have learned, in some parts of the Spanish-speaking world, people use **vos** in place of or in addition to **tú.** The **tú** and **vos** forms of the verb tener are very similar because they both end in **es.** However, in the **vos** form —**tenés**— the stress falls on the second syllable, and the first syllable contains only **e**, not **ie**. Listen to each sentence and indicate which form the speaker is using.

1. tú vos
2. tú vos
3. tú vos
4. tú vos
5. tú vos

Gramática

3. Sustantivos singulares y plurales: Using singular and plural nouns (Textbook p. 36)

01-17 Crucigrama. Complete the crossword puzzle with the opposite form of each word. If the word is in the singular, then write the plural form; if it is in the plural, then write the singular form.

1. alemán
2. francés
3. abril
4. japonés
5. problemas
6. jóvenes
7. nube
8. invierno
9. sol
10. universidad

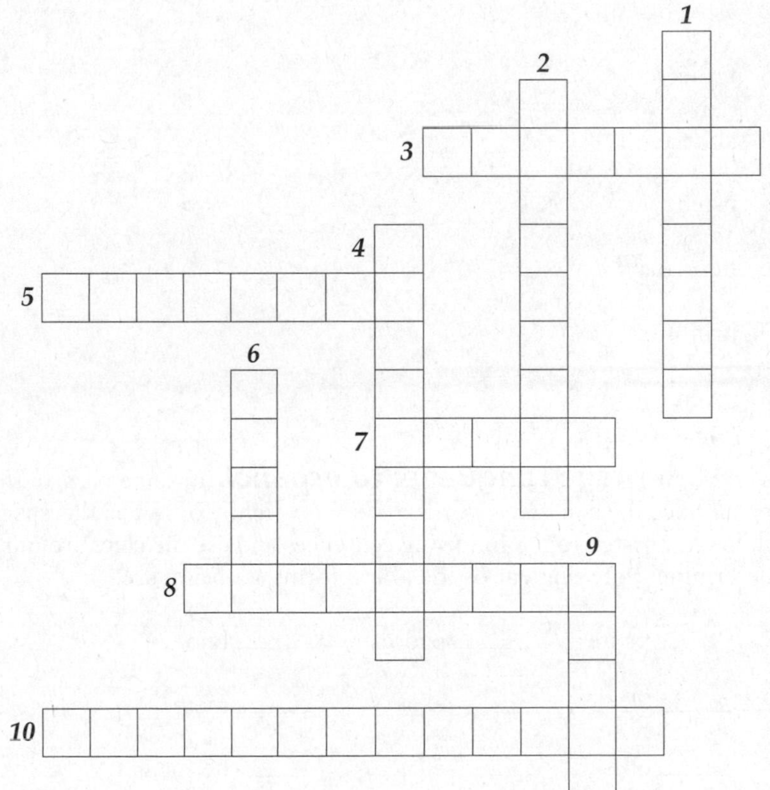

Nombre: ______________________ Fecha: ______________________

01-18 ¿Singular o plural? Listen as you hear each word stated and then select if it is singular or plural.

1. singular plural
2. singular plural
3. singular plural
4. singular plural
5. singular plural
6. singular plural
7. singular plural

01-19 Singular y plural. Pronounce each word, first in its singular form and then in its plural form. Pay special attention to your pronunciation of the vowel sounds.

1. estadounidense
2. español
3. francés
4. abuela
5. usted
6. hermana
7. primo
8. joven

01-20 Heritage Language: *tu español.* In some parts of the Spanish-speaking world, people often pronounce the **s** in many words either very lightly or not at all, especially when the **s** appears at the end of the word. Listen to the following sentences and use the clues around the words (like the verb conjugation) to determine if the singular or the plural forms are being used.

1. ______ padre ______ padres ______ hijo ______ hijos
2. ______ ella ______ ellas ______ nieto ______ nietos
3. ______ ella ______ ellas ______ hermana ______ hermanas
4. ______ usted ______ ustedes ______ madre ______ madres
5. ______ madre ______ madres ______ responsabilidad ______ responsabilidades

Nombre: ______________________ Fecha: ______________________

Gramática

4. El masculino y el femenino: Identifying masculine and feminine nouns (Textbook p. 37)

01-21 ¿Masculino o femenino? For each of the words you hear, select whether it is **masculino** or **femenino**.

1. masculino femenino
2. masculino femenino
3. masculino femenino
4. masculino femenino
5. masculino femenino
6. masculino femenino
7. masculino femenino
8. masculino femenino
9. masculino femenino
10. masculino femenino

01-22 Heritage Language: *tu español*. As you have learned, although many Spanish words ending in **a** are feminine words, some of them are masculine (and vice versa). Strengthen your understanding of the rules for determining the gender of nouns and reinforce your knowledge about exceptions to those rules by indicating if each word is masculine or feminine.

1. universidad	palabra masculina	palabra femenina
2. mapa	palabra masculina	palabra femenina
3. problema	palabra masculina	palabra femenina
4. computadora	palabra masculina	palabra femenina
5. moto	palabra masculina	palabra femenina
6. día	palabra masculina	palabra femenina
7. mano	palabra masculina	palabra femenina
8. programa	palabra masculina	palabra femenina
9. televisión	palabra masculina	palabra femenina
10. ciudad	palabra masculina	palabra femenina

Nombre: ______________________ Fecha: ______________________

Gramática

5. Los artículos definidos e indefinidos: Conveying *the, a, one,* and *some* (Textbook p. 38)

01-23 Los artículos definidos e indefinidos. In each sentence, select all of the definite and indefinite articles.

1. Tengo unos hermanos fabulosos.
2. La computadora de mi padre está en la oficina.
3. Hay una televisión en mi dormitorio.
4. Me gustan mucho los perros, pero no me gustan los gatos.
5. Todos los días escucho música. Prefiero escuchar la música rock.
6. Tengo una clase de español este semestre.

01-24 Los artículos.

Paso 1. Write the appropriate definite article for each noun. Be careful to be sure to use the correct masculine or feminine and singular or plural form.

1. ______________ fotos
2. ______________ abuela
3. ______________ libertades
4. ______________ mapa
5. ______________ prosperidad
6. ______________ moto
7. ______________ problemas
8. ______________ ciudades

Paso 2. Now write the appropriate indefinite article for each noun. Be careful to use the correct masculine or feminine and singular or plural form.

9. ______________ pizzas
10. ______________ hijo
11. ______________ recepción
12. ______________ mapas
13. ______________ problemas
14. ______________ hermanas
15. ______________ día
16. ______________ universidad
17. ______________ abuela
18. ______________ primo

01-25 Inventario. Listen as Pablo updates his mother on the inventory of their computer and electronics store. Write the definite and indefinite articles that he uses when referring to the following products. Pablo refers to each item twice, so be sure to write two responses for each. If no article is referenced, please write "x."

1. ______________ ______________ cables del Internet
2. ______________ ______________ teléfonos
3. ______________ ______________ computadoras
4. ______________ ______________ computadoras portátiles
5. ______________ ______________ calculadoras
6. ______________ ______________ teléfonos móviles

01-26 Una mochila (*bookbag*) perdida. Marga has just lost her bookbag, and it had a lot of important things inside. Complete the report of her missing items with the correct definite and indefinite articles. Be careful to choose the correct kind of article and to use the correct gender and number for each one.

En (1) ______________ mochila, Marga tiene

(2) ______________ computadora portátil (*portable*) y

(3) ______________ cámara digital. También tiene

(4) ______________ libro (*book*) de (5) ______________

profesora de su clase de español. (6) ______________ computadora

portátil tiene información importante, y (7) ______________ cámara

digital tiene (8) ______________ fotos especiales.

Nombre: ______________________________ Fecha: ______________________

01-27 Heritage Language: *tu español*. Indefinite articles do not correspond perfectly in Spanish and English. In English it is correct to state that "I have *a* car," but in Spanish the indefinite article is usually not used in this context unless you want to specify that you have only one car or unless you are also going to describe the car with an adjective after it. Thus, one says: "Tengo coche" or "Tengo un coche rápido." If you use the indefinite article without a description after the item ("Tengo un coche") then you are communicating that you have *one* car (instead of two or three). Listen to each sentence and then indicate which message the speaker has conveyed.

1. a family one family
2. a husband one husband
3. a son one son
4. a sister one sister
5. a mother one mother
6. a stepfather one stepfather

Comunicación II

Vocabulario

6. Gente: Giving details about yourself and others (Textbook p. 40)

01-28 ¿Quiénes son? For each person or group of people, choose the word or words that best describe them.

1. unos chicos unas niñas unas muchachas unas niñas

2. un chico una mujer un hombre una niña

3. unos niños unas señoras unos jóvenes unas muchachas

4. una muchacha un joven una mujer una niña

5. unos novios un niño una chica un muchacho

6. una mujer unos jóvenes un hombre unos niños

01-29 Las personas. Match each description with the appropriate term for the person being described.

1. la persona femenina que (*that*) es el amor (*love*) de una persona ______________
2. una persona femenina que tiene dieciséis años (*is 16 years old*) ______________
3. una persona masculina que tiene diecisiete años ______________
4. un adulto que tiene 50 años ______________
5. un joven que es el amor de una persona ______________
6. una adulta que tiene 40 años ______________

a. el hombre
b. la chica
c. la mujer
d. la novia
e. el chico
f. el novio

01-30 La gente. Using your new vocabulary, write the nouns that you would use to describe the following people **(chico, mujer,** etc).

1. Justin Timberlake ______________________________
2. Shakira ______________________________
3. Dakota Fanning ______________________________
4. Penélope Cruz ______________________________
5. Brad Pitt ______________________________

Nombre: ______________________ Fecha: ______________________

01-31 Heritage Language: *tu español.* The expressions you have learned to use in order to refer to people are used throughout the Spanish-speaking world. Just as in English, people from specific cultures and countries also use colloquial terms. Look up each word in the online dictionary of the Royal Academy of the Spanish Language (http://buscon.rae.es), and write one vocabulary word you have learned from your textbook that has the same or a very similar meaning.

1. chaval ______________________
2. chamaco ______________________
3. chama ______________________
4. moza ______________________
5. pibe ______________________
6. chiquilla ______________________
7. crío ______________________

Gramática

7. Los adjetivos posesivos: Stating possession (Textbook p. 41)

01-32 Nuestras familias. Write the correct possessive adjective for each family member.

MODELO madrastra (yo) *mi*
hijas (nosotros) *nuestras*

1. hermana (usted) ______________
2. abuelos (yo) ______________
3. padre (ella) ______________
4. primos (ustedes) ______________
5. padrastro (tú) ______________
6. familias (nosotros) ______________
7. tía (yo) ______________
8. tíos (tú) ______________
9. madre (nosotros) ______________
10. abuelos (usted) ______________

01-33 La familia de Antonio. Listen as Antonio describes his family and then, using the word bank as a spelling guide for the names you hear, complete the following answers to the questions. Use possessive adjectives in order to avoid repeating evident information from the question.

Antonio	Arcadio	Carlos	Clara	David
Gabriela	Lucía	Pablo	Pedro	Violeta

MODELO ¿Cómo se llama (*What is the name of*) la esposa de Antonio?
Su esposa se llama (*is named*) *Violeta*.

1. ¿Cómo se llaman los hermanos de Antonio?

   ________________ hermanos se llaman ________________ y ________________.

2. ¿Cómo se llama el esposo de Marta?

   ________________ esposo se llama ________________.

3. ¿Cómo se llaman los hijos de Marta?

   ________________ hijos se llaman ________________ y ________________.

4. ¿Cómo se llama la esposa de Arcadio?

   ________________ esposa se llama ________________.

5. ¿Cómo se llaman los hijos de Arcadio?

   ________________ hijos se llaman ________________ y ________________.

6. ¿Cómo se llaman los abuelos de Gabriela?

   ________________ abuelos se llaman ________________ y ________________.

Nombre: ______________________ Fecha: ______________________

01-34 ¿De quién es? Look at the pictures and captions, and then use possessive adjectives to indicate to whom each item belongs.

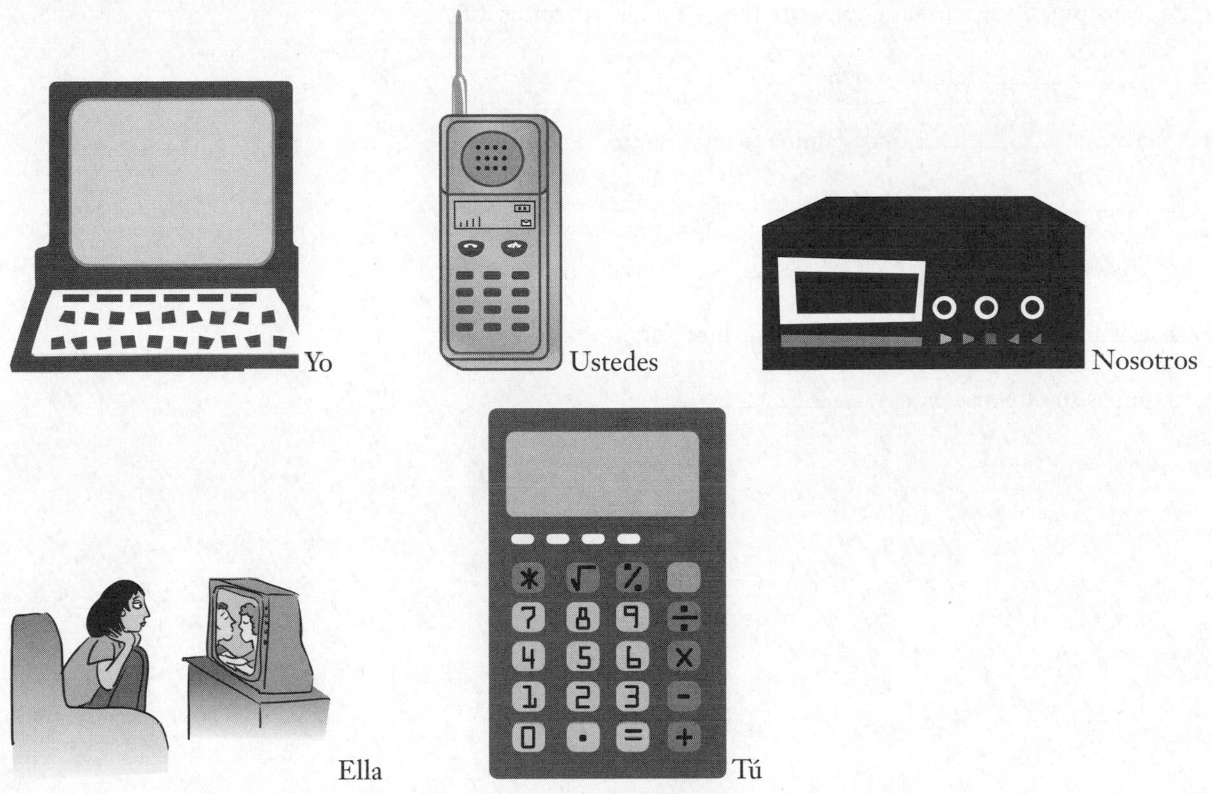

1. Es ______________ calculadora.
2. Es ______________ computadora.
3. Es ______________ radio.
4. Es ______________ teléfono móvil (*cell phone*).
5. Es ______________ televisor.

01-35 ¿Y tu familia? Follow the steps to introduce your family to a friend.

Paso 1. Jot down the names of the family members you would like to introduce. Provide the word in Spanish that describes your relationship to them as well as the corresponding possessive adjective. Be sure that your words agree with the gender and number of your family members.

MODELO Patrick Genoa, mi abuelo

____

____

____

Paso 2. Your new friend is meeting your family for the first time. Using the information from Paso 1, introduce each person.

01-36 Heritage Language: *tu español.* It is often difficult to remember when to use accents. The word **mi** that you have learned is pronounced exactly the same as the word **mí**, but when the **i** has a written accent, it means **me**. For each sentence write the correct word: **mi** or **mí**.

1. ____________________ familia es fabulosa.
2. Para (*for*) ____________________ la familia es importante.
3. ____________________ hermana tiene veinte años (*is twenty years old*).
4. El libro (*book*) es para ____________________.
5. Me gusta ____________________ profesor de literatura.
6. Las vitaminas son buenas para ____________________.

Gramática

8. Los adjetivos descriptivos: Supplying details about people, places, and things (Textbook p. 43)

01-37 Nuestras características físicas. Match each word with its opposite.

1. delgado ______________	a. pequeña
2. baja ______________	b. débil
3. guapo ______________	c. alta
4. fuerte ______________	d. gordo
5. grande ______________	e. feo

01-38 Las características físicas de los famosos.

Paso 1. Select the adjective that best describes the famous people listed.

1. Cameron Díaz	alta	gorda
2. Salma Hayek	grande	guapa
3. Ricky Martin	pequeño	alto
4. Shakira	pequeña	fea
5. Salma Hayek y Shakira	bonitas	feas
6. Enrique Iglesias y Ricky Martin	delgados	gordos

Paso 2. Use the adjectives you chose for each item above and the correct form of the verb **ser** to write one sentence about the famous people listed.

7. Cameron Díaz ______________.
8. Salma Hayek ______________.
9. Ricky Martin ______________.
10. Shakira Mebarak ______________.
11. Shakira Mebarak y Salma Hayek ______________.
12. Enrique Iglesias y Ricky Martin ______________.

01-39 Nuestras personalidades. Complete the crossword puzzle with the correct opposite of each adjective.

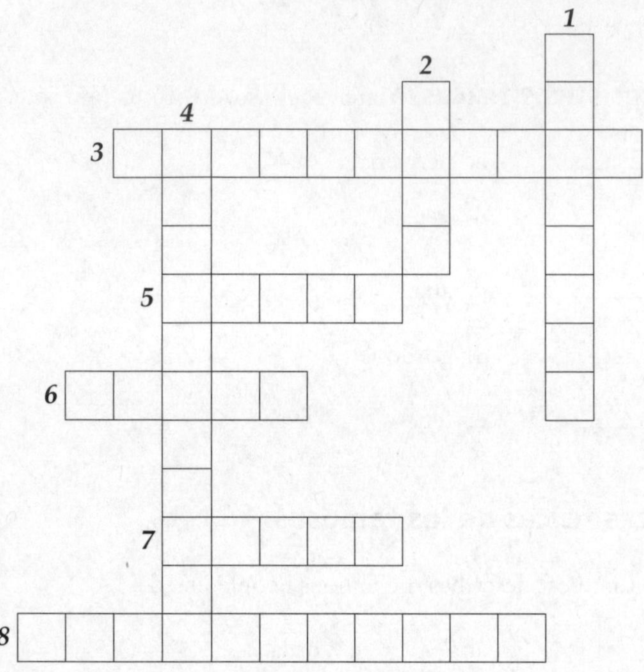

1. trabajador
2. bueno
3. perezosa
4. irresponsable
5. rica
6. inteligente
7. mala
8. aburrido

Nombre: ______________________ Fecha: ______________________

01-40 ¿Cómo son tú y tus amigos? Think about yourself and three of your closest friends.

Paso 1. Take notes on adjectives that describe each of you.

1. Yo
   Características físicas / Personalidad:
   ____
   ____

2. Mi amigo/a
   Características físicas / Personalidad:
   ____
   ____

3. Mi amigo/a
   Características físicas / Personalidad:
   ____
   ____

4. Mi amigo/a
   Características físicas / Personalidad:
   ____
   ____

Paso 2. Now write a paragraph describing you and your friends. Try to use the correct forms of the verb **ser** throughout your description, and also to make your adjectives agree in both number and gender with the person or people described.

____
____
____
____
____
____
____
____
____
____

Nombre: ______________________ Fecha: ______________________

01-41 ¿Cómo son? You are studying abroad, and you take the following photograph during a gathering that your host family organizes. Using the vocabulary and verbs that you have learned so far, and the useful expressions provided, write a description of your host family. You should indicate what their nationality is, give each person a name, describe their relationships, use some of their physical characteristics to make it clear who each person is in the photograph, and also mention some of their personality traits.

una comida – *a meal, a luncheon*	mucha comida deliciosa – *plenty of delicious food, a lot of delicious food*
una fiesta – *a party*	el aniversario – *the anniversary*
el cumpleaños – *the birthday*	

____

____

____

____

____

____

____

____

____

____

____

____

____

____

Nombre: ______________________________ Fecha: ______________________

01-42 Heritage Language: *tu español*. Vocabulary often varies from one region to another in most languages; the Spanish language is especially rich with such variety. Look up the following words in Appendix 3 **También se dice** of your textbook and match each word to its closest equivalent.

1. musculoso ________________ a. simpática
2. graciosa ________________ b. delgado
3. hermoso ________________ c. cómica
4. amable ________________ d. fuerte
5. flaco ________________ e. guapo

Nota cultural: El español, lengua diversa (Textbook p. 46)

01-43 Lenguas diversas. Based on what you have learned in **Capítulo 1** about the diversity of the Spanish and English languages, answer the following questions.

1. What kind of variations in the English language does your textbook mention?

____

____

2. What different accents of native speakers of English from the United States can you distinguish and easily identify?

____

____

3. What different accents of native speakers of English from outside the United States can you distinguish and easily identify?

____

____

4. If you were to visit another English-speaking country, how much difficulty would you have communicating with the people that live there? Why?

____

____

5. In what ways are both Spanish and English "diverse" languages?

____

____

01-44 ¿Cómo se dice? Based on the cultural information in **Capítulo 1**, answer the following questions.

1. According to the textbook, what are three ways that people in different parts of the United States use to refer to soft drinks?

____

____

2. According to your dictionary (or an on-line dictionary), what does each of those words mean? Is "soft drink" one of the first definitions of those words?

____

____

3. According to the textbook, what are three different ways that native speakers of Spanish use to describe someone as "funny"?

____

____

4. According to your dictionary, what does each of those words mean? Is "funny" one of the first definitions that appears?

____

____

5. According to the textbook, what are three different ways to refer to a bus in Spanish?

____

____

6. Do all of those words appear in your dictionary? If so, according to your reference source, what does each of those words mean?

____

____

7. How will your awareness of the diversity of the Spanish language throughout the world influence your approach to studying the language and to trying to communicate in the language?

____

____

Vocabulario

9. Los números 31 a 100: Counting from 31 to 100 (Textbook p. 47)

01-45 Números de teléfono. Listen to Cristina's friends' phone numbers and write them as you would a 7-digit number in the United States. Follow the model closely.

MODELO su abuela Marta *254-9733*

1. sus hermanos Roberto y Raúl ______________
2. su amigo Tomás ______________
3. sus primas Emilia y Rudi ______________
4. su hermana Raquel ______________
5. su madre ______________
6. su abuelo José ______________

01-46 Matemáticas. Give the following math equations and their solutions (plus = **más**, minus = **menos**, times = **por**, divided by = **dividido por**, equals = **son**).

1. 52 + 24 =
2. 4 × 11 =
3. 36 ÷ 3 =
4. 20 × 4 =
5. 60 ÷ 5 =
6. 6 × 12 =
7. 67 – 9 =
8. 78 + 5 =

01-47 Matemáticas. Listen to the math equations and write their solutions in numerals.

1. ______________
2. ______________
3. ______________
4. ______________
5. ______________
6. ______________

Nombre: ______________________________ Fecha: ______________________

01-48 Heritage Language: *tu español.*

Paso 1. Temperaturas. Listen to the report about the weather in Latin America on a Spanish-speaking radio station in the United States and write the correct temperature for each city.

1. Santiago, Chile ________________ °F
2. Bariloche, Argentina ________________ °F
3. San Vicente, El Salvador ________________ °F
4. La Esperanza, Honduras ________________ °F
5. Barranca, Perú ________________ °F
6. Cartagena, Colombia ________________ °F

Paso 2. Conversión de temperaturas. While in the United States people are accustomed to discussing temperatures in degrees Fahrenheit, in most of the Spanish-speaking world, people talk about degrees Celsius or **centígrados.** As a result, it can be confusing when discussing the weather with family or friends who are in other countries. Use the conversion to translate each temperature to its approximate equivalent in degrees Celsius and then describe the weather for each place using the expressions: **hace calor, hace buen tiempo,** or **hace frío.**

CONVERSIÓN DE TEMPERATURAS

35°C = 95°F

30°C = 86°F

25°C = 77°F

20°C =68°F

15°C = 59°F

10°C =50°F

5°C = 41°F

0°C = 32°F

7. Santiago, Chile ________________ °C ________________________.
8. Bariloche, Argentina ________________ °C ________________________.
9. San Vicente, El Salvador ________________ °C ________________________.
10. La Esperanza, Honduras ________________ °C ________________________.
11. Barranca, Perú ________________ °C ________________________.
12. Cartagena, Colombia ________________ °C ________________________.

Nombre: ______________________ Fecha: ______________________

Escucha (Textbook p. 49)

01-49 Los novios y sus familias. Esperanza and Martín are dating, and Esperanza is talking about how different their families are.

Paso 1. Before listening, write down some words that you think you might hear her say.

____

____

____

____

Paso 2. Now listen to Esperanza and write all of the words from Paso 1 that she actually says.

____

____

01-50 Las diferencias y las familias.

Paso 1

1. Listen to Esperanza's comparison of her family and Martín's family and select all of the words that you hear.

________ similares	________ pobres
________ primos	________ formal
________ aburrida	________ grande
________ inteligente	________ gusta
________ vuestra	________ fortuna
________ abuelos	________ elegantes

Paso 2. Las familias de Esperanza y Martín. Now indicate if the following statements are **cierto** or **falso.** If necessary, listen to the passage one more time.

2. La familia de Esperanza es muy grande. cierto falso
3. La familia de Esperanza es rica. cierto falso
4. Los hermanos de Esperanza son antipáticos. cierto falso
5. La familia de Martín es pobre. cierto falso
6. La familia de Esperanza es formal. cierto falso
7. La familia de Martín es un poco aburrida. cierto falso

Nombre: ______________________ Fecha: ______________________

¡Conversemos! (Textbook p. 50)

01-51 Nuestras familias y amigos. Contact a fellow student in order to discuss friends and family. Use the verb **tener** to tell the person about the friends and family you have, and use the verb **ser** to describe at least two physical characteristics and at least two personality traits for each person you mention. You should share information about at least ten people. Use **tener, ser,** and the vocabulary that you have learned to ask your partner questions about his or her friends and family. In preparation for your conversation, write at least five questions in Spanish that you plan to ask your partner.

1. ______________________
2. ______________________
3. ______________________
4. ______________________
5. ______________________

Nombre: ______________________________ Fecha: ______________________

Escribe (Textbook p. 50)

01-52 Asociaciones y características. Think about the people in your life who are closest to you and choose four to focus on for the following writing activity.

Paso 1. For each person, write down some words in Spanish that you associate with him or her. These can be adjectives that describe the person's personality or physical traits, or they can be things that the person likes. Try to write as many words as possible for each person.

1. ____

____

____

2. ____

____

____

3. ____

____

____

4. ____

____

____

Paso 2. Letras y palabras. Choose two of the people you considered for the previous activity and using each person's first name, middle name, nickname or last name, write key words (descriptive nouns or adjectives) that begin with each letter of the name.

5. ______________________	6. ______________________
______________________	______________________
______________________	______________________
______________________	______________________
______________________	______________________
______________________	______________________
______________________	______________________
______________________	______________________

Paso 3. Frases. Now build phrases around each word using **tener, ser, gustar,** and any other useful expressions that you have learned.

7. ______________________ 8. ______________________

Cultura: Los Estados Unidos (Textbook pp. 52–53)

01-53 Estados Unidos. Based on what you learned about Hispanics in the United States in Capítulo 1, match each person and place with the word or phrase most closely associated with it.

1. Cristina Saralegui ______
2. Nueva York ______
3. Albert Pujols ______
4. Miami ______
5. St. Augustine ______
6. México ______

a. Ciudad fundada en 1565
b. Celebración de la herencia puertorriqueña
c. Mucha influencia en Estados Unidos
d. Ciudad con la población más grande de hispanos en Estados Unidos
e. Origen del grupo de hispanos más grande de Estados Unidos
f. Béisbol

Nombre: ______________________________ Fecha: ______________________

01-54 Vistas culturales: Estados Unidos. View the video segments in order to complete each part of the activity. You will likely not understand all of the words that you hear, but you should relax because you are capable of understanding more than enough to be able to respond to the questions without difficulty.

Estados Unidos: Introducción. Read the questions, then watch the video and then select the correct answer or answers to each question.

1. Según (*according to*) el video, ¿qué porcentaje de la población de los Estados Unidos es hispano?

   ______ 2,5%   ______ 5%

   ______ 12,5%   ______ 15%

2. ¿Cuántos países tienen una población hispana más grande que la población hispana de los Estados Unidos?

   ______ 1   ______ 3

   ______ 2   ______ 4

3. ¿De dónde son los grupos más grandes (*largest*) de inmigrantes en los Estados Unidos?

   ______ México   ______ Puerto Rico

   ______ Argentina   ______ Cuba

   ______ España

4. Según el video, ¿de qué país es el 66% de los hispanos en los Estados Unidos?

   ______ Cuba   ______ México

   ______ Argentina   ______ Puerto Rico

5. Según el video, ¿en qué ciudades estadounidenses es especialmente evidente la influencia de los hispanos?

   ______ Los Ángeles

   ______ Santa Fe

   ______ San Francisco

   ______ San Antonio

   ______ San Diego

La comida hispana. Read the questions, watch the video and then select with which place each food item is associated according to the narrator.

6. mole

   a. México   b. Puerto Rico   c. Venezuela

7. piraguas

   a. México   b. Puerto Rico   c. Venezuela

8. bacalaitos

   a. México   b. Puerto Rico   c. Venezuela

9. arepas

   a. México   b. Puerto Rico   c. Venezuela

10. tostones

   a. México   b. Puerto Rico   c. Venezuela

El arte hispano. Read the questions, watch the video and then select the correct response or responses to each question.

11. ¿En qué ciudades estadounidenses tiene especial importancia el muralismo?

    _____ San Francisco

    _____ San Antonio

    _____ El Paso

    _____ Nueva York

12. ¿Con qué grupo indígena se asocian los orígenes del arte muralista?

    _____ Los mayas

    _____ Los aztecas

    _____ Los aymara

    _____ Los incas

13. ¿En qué ciudad hay murales indígenas?

    _____ Los Ángeles

    _____ Miami

    _____ Bonampak

    _____ El Paso

14. ¿Qué representan muchos murales?

    _____ historia

    _____ animales

    _____ plantas

    _____ literatura

Los deportes. Read the questions, watch the video, and then, based on the information in the video, select with which sport each place or person is associated.

15. Cuba

    a. béisbol b. jai alai c. boxeo

16. República Dominicana

    a. béisbol b. jai alai c. boxeo

17. Roberto Clemente

    a. béisbol b. jai alai c. boxeo

18. José Canseco

    a. béisbol b. jai alai c. boxeo

19. Alex Rodríguez

    a. béisbol b. jai alai c. boxeo

20. Fernando Vargas

    a. béisbol b. jai alai c. boxeo

21. Florida

    a. béisbol b. jai alai c. boxeo

22. España

    a. béisbol b. jai alai c. boxeo

Nombre: ______________________ Fecha: ______________________

Más cultura

01-55 Las familias hispanas. Read the following information about Hispanic families and then answer the questions, comparing them to your own concept of family.

- El concepto de la familia en muchas culturas del mundo hispano incluye (*includes*) más que la familia inmediata. La familia extendida —los primos, los tíos, y los abuelos— puede ser tan (*can be just as*) importante como la familia inmediata— los hermanos, los padres y los hijos—. Muchas personas se reúnen con (*get together with*) la familia extendida con mucha frecuencia.
- En muchas culturas del mundo hispano, las familias tratan (*treat*) a las personas mayores (*older*) con mucho respeto y admiración. Las personas mayores son muy importantes en la familia. Por sus experiencias, tienen muchos conocimientos y sabiduría (*knowledge and wisdom*) para ofrecerles (*offer*) a las personas más jóvenes de la familia.
- Otras personas importantes en las familias hispanas cristianas son los padrinos (*godparents*). Es posible tener como padrinos a tíos o a otras personas de la familia. También se puede (*one can*) tener como padrinos a los muy buenos amigos. En algunas familias, los padrinos participan en la educación religiosa y moral de los niños, en otras tienen un rol más simbólico. Siempre es un gran honor ser el padrino o la madrina de un niño.

1. How important do you feel your extended family is in your life? In what ways does the importance of your extended family (or lack thereof) manifest itself in the way you choose to live your life and make important decisions?

   ____

2. How often do you get together with your cousins, aunts, uncles, and grandparents? Would you like to get together more frequently? Why or why not?

   ____

3. Can you imagine gathering for a meal with many members of your family every week or once every month?

   ____

4. How much do you value the opinions of older people in your family?

   ____

5. Do you have godparents or people in your life that serve a similar role? What are the benefits of having those people as part of your personal support system?

   ____

6. In these areas of family practices and perspectives, do you think your case is similar to those of your friends? Do you think it's representative of many people across the United States? Why or why not?

   ____

01-56 Heritage Language: *tu mundo hispano*. Interview at least three people of Spanish-speaking heritage in order to find out about their own concepts of family. If you are of Spanish-speaking heritage, at least two people should be from outside of your own family.

Paso 1. Write at least five questions that you will ask the people you plan to interview. The following are some ideas to consider while formulating your questions: what kind of relationship they have with their immediate and extended family; what their attitudes are toward older family members, gender roles, and family meals; and whether or not they believe their own customs are similar to those of people throughout their culture.

1. ______________________________
2. ______________________________
3. ______________________________
4. ______________________________
5. ______________________________

Paso 2. Write a brief description in English of the results of your interviews and how they have impacted your own understanding of Hispanic family practices.

____

____

____

____

____

Nombre: ______________________________ Fecha: ______________________

Ambiciones siniestras

Episodio 1

Lectura: *Conexiones* (Textbook p. 54)

01-57 ¿Comprendes? Using the words provided, complete the statements based on the reading in **Capítulo 1.** You may use each word only once.

aburrida	simpáticas	trabajador	perezoso	simpático	feo	hermanas	guapas
gordo	difícil	guapo	interesantes	cómico	jóvenes		

1. Las clases de Alejandra son ____________________.
2. En la opinión de Alejandra, Manolo es ____________________, ____________________ y ____________________.
3. Manolo tiene dos ____________________.
4. En la opinión de Eduardo, Cisco es ____________________.
5. La clase de Macroeconomía de Eduardo es ____________________ y ____________________.
6. Las mujeres que le gustan a "elrico" son ____________________, ____________________, y ____________________.
7. En la opinión de Lupe, "elrico" probablemente es ____________________, ____________________, y ____________________.

Video: *¿Quiénes son?* (Textbook p. 56)

01-58 ¿Quiénes son? The title of the episode of **Ambiciones Siniestras** for **Capítulo 1** is **¿Quiénes son?**. Based on that title and the following still shots from the episode, write a brief account of what you think this episode will be about, and what kinds of words you think the characters will use.

____

____

____

____

____

____

01-59 Escucha bien. As you watch the episode, mark the words that you hear used in the conversations.

____________ universidad	____________ pizarra
____________ chico	____________ tíos
____________ gracias	____________ hablar
____________ niño	____________ hermanos
____________ comprendo	____________ hola
____________ escucha	____________ familia
____________ encantado	

Nombre: ______________________ Fecha: ______________________

01-60 Comprensión general. Answer the questions about the main events of the episode by selecting **sí** or **no.** If necessary, view the episode again.

1. Did Cisco end up helping Eduardo with his Macro homework? sí no
2. Do Lupe and Marisol know each other when the episode begins? sí no
3. Do Marisol and Phillip seem to get along well? sí no
4. Does Lupe seem to dislike him? sí no
5. Does Philip seem to like Marisol and Lupe? sí no
6. Do Manolo and Alejandra seem to be good friends? sí no

01-61 Los detalles. Complete the following statements using the words provided.

simpático	estadounidense	buena
guapo	interesante	

1. En la opinión de Cisco, la clase de macroeconomía es ______________.
2. En su opinión, el profesor de la clase es ______________.
3. Lupe es ______________.
4. En la opinión de Lupe, Phillip es ______________.
5. En la opinión de Marisol, Phillip es ______________.

01-62 Hipótesis. Consider the following questions about the reading and the video from **Capítulo 1,** and then write a description in English of what you think might happen in the next episodes.

How do you think the relationships between Lupe, Marisol and Phillip will develop? What do you think might happen with Manolo and Alejandra? Do you think Lupe will respond to the mysterious e-mail message she received? Why or why not? Who do you think sent her the message? Why do you think the person sent her the message?

____

____

____

____

____

____

Comunidades

01-63 Experiential Learning: Familias famosas. Choose a famous Hispanic person and research the person and his or her family. Prepare a presentation for class in which you describe the person and also present his or her family tree. Some people to consider researching are Martin Sheen, Soledad O'Brien, Jimmy Smits, Cameron Díaz, Benicio del Toro, Princess Letizia Ortiz of Asturias, and King Juan Carlos I of Spain.

01-64 Service Learning: Familia, cultura y niños. Contact your local public library and volunteer to organize and hold a special Hispanic-themed story time event for children in your area. Find one or two books from your library's collection that relate to Hispanic culture and family practices (for example, *In My Family* by Carmen Lomas Garza, *Family Pictures* by Carmen Lomas Garza, or *Family, Familia* by Diane Gonzales Bertrand, Pauline Rodríguez Howard and Julia Mercedes Castilla). If your library does not have any such holdings, recommend that they acquire books of this kind and hold a fundraiser with your Spanish class in order to buy at least one of them and donate it to your library.

Nombre: ______________________ Fecha: ______________________

2 La vida universitaria

Comunicación I

Vocabulario

1. Las materias y las especialidades: Sharing information about courses and majors (Textbook p. 62)

02-01 ¿Qué aprenden los estudiantes en las clases? Using your understanding of cognates, match the topics below with the classes in which you would most likely learn about them.

1. la informática __D__
2. la literatura __F__
3. el periodismo __E__
4. la música __A__
5. la arquitectura __H__
6. los idiomas __G__
7. el derecho __J__
8. la administración de empresas __C__
9. las matemáticas __B__
10. la biología __I__

a. el piano o la guitarra
b. las ecuaciones diferenciales
c. el dinero y la economía
d. las computadoras
e. cómo escribir artículos
f. los poemas y las novelas
g. el vocabulario, la gramática y la cultura
h. la construcción de las casas
i. las plantas y los animales
j. la legislación

Nombre: ______________________ Fecha: ______________________

02-02 ¿Qué clases tienen? Using your understanding of cognates and based on each student's major, identify which class each person is taking.

inteligencia artificial	anatomía humana
introducción al fotoperiodismo	el cubismo y el surrealismo
derecho constitucional	introducción a la literatura hispanoamericana
finanzas de las empresas multinacionales	tecnología educativa

1. La especialidad de Pablo es administración de empresas; tiene una clase de finanzas de las empresas multinacional.
2. La especialidad de Mariana y Yolanda es medicina; tienen una clase de anatomia humana.
3. La especialidad de Antonio y Ana es informática; tienen una clase de inteligencia artifical.
4. La especialidad de Marta es español; tiene una clase de introducción a la literatura hispano-americana.
5. La especialidad de Adriana y Pedro es pedagogía; tienen una clase de techologia educative.
6. La especialidad de Enrique y Lucía es periodismo; tienen una clase de introduccion al fotoperiodism.
7. La especialidad de José Luis es arte; tiene una clase de El cubismo y el surrealismo.
8. La especialidad de Javier y María es derecho; tienen una clase de derecho constitucional.

02-03 Personas famosas. Identify the class in which you would most likely study the following famous people or their work.

1. Bill Gates B
2. Pablo Picasso e
3. Luciano Pavarotti D
4. Shakespeare F
5. Frida Kahlo G
6. Frank Lloyd Wright A
7. Emily Dickinson C

a. arquitectura moderna
b. introducción a la informática I: Software básico
c. poesía norteamericana
d. introducción a la ópera: grandes tenores y sopranos
e. arte moderno español
f. literatura inglesa
g. arte moderno mexicano

Nombre: ______________________ Fecha: ______________________

02-04 ¿Qué clases tomas tú?

Paso 1. Fill out the following form with information about yourself and your studies this semester.

1. Nombre y apellidos (*last names*): ______________________
2. Especialidad: ______________________
3. Número total de créditos este semestre: ______________________
4. Clases de este semestre:

   ____

   ____

5. Clase favorita: ______________________
6. La clase más interesante: ______________________
7. La clase más aburrida: ______________________

Paso 2. Now introduce yourself, identify your major and the classes you are taking, and share your opinion about your classes.

02-05 Heritage Language: *tu español*. Because some Spanish terms associated with educational settings look quite similar to other terms in English, it easy to forget which words are cognates and which are false cognates. Avoid making mistakes with the following words by looking them up in a dictionary and then selecting the correct definition of each term.

1. colegio
   a. elementary school
   b. high school
   c. college or university

2. bachillerato
   a. elementary school studies
   b. high school studies
   c. undergraduate university degree

3. licenciatura
   a. part of elementary school studies
   b. part of high school studies
   c. university degree

4. facultad
   a. professor
   b. academic subdivision (as in a college or school) within a university
   c. university degree

5. doctorado
   a. part of elementary school studies
   b. part of high school studies
   c. university degree

Nombre: ______________________ Fecha: ______________________

Pronunciación: Word stress and accent marks (Textbook p. 63)

In Spanish, written accents are used to distinguish word meaning, or when a word is "breaking" a pronunciation rule. Here are the basic rules of Spanish pronunciation and accentuation.

1. Words ending in a vowel, or in the consonants **n** or **s** are stressed on the *next-to-last syllable*. Listen to and then pronounce the following words.

   medi**ci**na, de**re**cho, **gran**de, **tie**nen, a**bue**los, no**so**tros, **ar**te

2. Words ending in consonants other than **n** or **s** are stressed on the *last syllable*. Listen to and then pronounce the following words.

   te**ner**, us**ted**, Rafa**el**, ciu**dad**, Ga**briel**, fe**liz**, lle**gar**

3. All words "breaking" rules #1 and #2 above need a written accent on the stressed syllable. Listen to and then pronounce the following words.

   televisi**ón**, biolo**gí**a, infor**má**tica, **fá**cil, Ra**món**, **mú**sica

4. Written accents are used on all *interrogative* and *exclamatory* words. Listen to and then pronounce the following words.

   ¿**Có**mo?, ¿**Qué**?, ¿**Cuán**do?, ¿**Quién**?, ¿**Cuán**tos?, ¿**Dón**de?, ¡**Qué** bueno!

5. Written accents are also used to *differentiate meaning* of certain one-syllable words that are written and pronounced alike. Listen to and then pronounce the following words.

él (*he*)	el (*the*)	**sí** (*yes*)	si (*if*)
mí (*me*)	mi (*my*)	**tú** (*you*)	tu (*your*)

02-06 ¿Qué dice? Listen to each word and then select the spelling that corresponds with what you heard.

1. hablo	habló	4. separo	separó
2. trabajara	trabajará	5. contestara	contestará
3. llevo	llevó	6. estudio	estudió

02-07 Pronunciación y acentos.

Paso 1. Review the words below and select the syllable where the natural stress would fall according to the rules you have learned in this chapter.

1. mu si ca	5. bo rra dor	9. fe liz
2. ma te ma ti cas	6. u ni ver si dad	10. com po si cion
3. bo li gra fo	7. la piz	
4. di ver si dad	8. e xa men	

Nombre: ______________________________ Fecha: ______________________

Paso 2. Now listen to the pronunciation of the words. Compare the pronunciation that you hear with the natural stress that you identified in **Paso 1.** Finally, decide which words require a written accent and write each word correctly.

11. ____________________
12. ____________________
13. ____________________
14. ____________________
15. ____________________
16. ____________________
17. ____________________
18. ____________________
19. ____________________
20. ____________________

02-08 Correcciones. Test your knowledge of how accents and word stress work in Spanish. Listen to each word and then write it, making certain to use written accents when needed.

1. ____________________
2. ____________________
3. ____________________
4. ____________________
5. ____________________
6. ____________________

Nota cultural: Las universidades hispanas (Textbook p. 64)

02-09 Las universidades hispanas. Answer the following questions based on the information in your textbook.

1. How do the curricular requirements of your degree program at your university compare to those of a student at a university in the Spanish-speaking world?

____

____

2. How do the housing options on your campus compare to those of most universities in the Spanish-speaking world?

____

____

3. Where do most students attending your university choose to live? How does this compare to students in the Spanish-speaking world?

____

____

4. What kinds of extracurricular activities are available to students at your university? How do these compare to activities available at many universities in the Spanish-speaking world?

____

____

Vocabulario

2. La sala de clase: Describing your classroom and classmates (Textbook p. 65)

02-10 ¿Cuáles son las palabras asociadas? Study the words in each group and select the one that does not belong.

1. la pizarra	el borrador	la ventana	la tiza
2. la pared	el bolígrafo	el papel	el lápiz
3. la silla	el escritorio	el idioma	la mesa
4. la puerta	la ventana	la pared	la música
5. los apuntes	el bolígrafo	el cuaderno	la puerta
6. la mochila	la compañera	el libro	el cuaderno

Nombre: ______________________ Fecha: ______________________

02-15 Una semana típica de Amaya.

Paso 1. Listen to the telephone conversation between Amaya and her mother. Then indicate which activities correspond to the days of Amaya's typical week.

1. tener clase

   ________ los lunes, los miércoles y los viernes

   ________ los martes y los jueves

   ________ todos los días de la semana

2. trabajar

   ________ los lunes, los miércoles y los viernes

   ________ los martes y los jueves

   ________ todos los días de la semana

3. comer en la cafetería

   ________ los lunes, los miércoles y los viernes

   ________ los martes y los jueves

   ________ todos los días de la semana

4. estudiar

   ________ los lunes, los miércoles y los viernes

   ________ los martes y los jueves

   ________ todos los días de la semana

5. contestar e-mails

   ________ los lunes, los miércoles y los viernes

   ________ los martes y los jueves

   ________ todos los días de la semana

6. hablar con las amigas

   ________ los lunes, los miércoles y los viernes

   ________ los martes y los jueves

   ________ todos los días de la semana

Paso 2. Listen to the conversation again and indicate which activities Amaya does alone and which activities she does with Enrique. In some cases, Amaya does the activity alone as well as with Enrique.

7. tener clase — Amaya ________ Amaya y Enrique juntos ________
8. trabajar — Amaya ________ Amaya y Enrique juntos ________
9. comer — Amaya ________ Amaya y Enrique juntos ________
10. estudiar — Amaya ________ Amaya y Enrique juntos ________
11. contestar e-mails — Amaya ________ Amaya y Enrique juntos ________
12. hablar con las amigas — Amaya ________ Amaya y Enrique juntos ________

02-16 ¿Cómo es mi universidad? Complete the following paragraph about university life by choosing the correct form of the appropriate verb.

En mi universidad, normalmente los estudiantes (1) (toman / tomas / comprenden / comprendes) entre (*between*) cuatro y seis clases cada semestre. Algunos (*some*) estudiantes (2) (estudiamos / estudian / trabajamos / trabajan) en una tienda (*store*) o en la librería (*bookstore*) también porque ellos (3) (necesita / necesitan / compra / compran) dinero.

Mis amigos y yo (4) (esperamos / esperan / vivimos / viven) en una de las residencias estudiantiles del campus, pero otros prefieren estar en un apartamento. Yo (5) (aprende / aprendo / comprende / comprendo) su preferencia porque la comida (*food*) en nuestras cafeterías no es muy buena –¡a veces (*sometimes*) es horrible!

02-17 Comparación y contraste. Compare Marta and her friends to yourself and your friends.

Paso 1. For each affirmation, compare yourself to Marta and her friends by stating whether or not you and your friends have similar habits.

1. Marta trabaja en un restaurante.

____

2. Marta y sus amigas viven en una residencia estudiantil.

____

3. Marta recibe buenas notas.

____

4. Marta y sus amigos comen en la cafetería de la universidad.

____

5. Marta toma cinco clases este semestre.

____

6. Marta y sus hermanos comen con sus padres todos los domingos.

____

Paso 2. Using the information above, describe the things that you have in common with Marta and her friends, and the things that you do not have in common. Be careful to use the correct forms of the verbs.

Nombre: ______________________________ Fecha: ______________________

02-18 Heritage Language: *tu español.*

Paso 1. In some parts of the Spanish-speaking world, people often pronounce the **s** in many words either very lightly or not at all, especially when the **s** appears at the end of the word. As a result, it can be easy to forget to include the **s** when writing those words. Listen to the following sentences and use the clues around the words in order to determine if the speaker is talking about **tú** or if the person is referring to **ella** or **él** and select which spelling of the word is correct.

1. estudias estudia
2. lees lee
3. enseñas enseña
4. necesitas necesita
5. corres corre

Paso 2. In some parts of the Spanish-speaking world, people use **vos** in place of or in addition to **tú**. These forms are easily distinguished in speech because of the syllable that is stressed. However, the conjugation of regular **-ar** and **-er** verbs in the **vos** form is written exactly the same as the **tú** form, with the exception of a written accent on the last vowel. Because of this close similarity, when one is writing it can be easy to forget to include the accent. Listen to each sentence and indicate which spelling of the word is correct.

6. preparas preparás
7. aprendes aprendés
8. regresas regresás
9. corres corrés
10. comprendes comprendés

Gramática

4. La formación de preguntas y las palabras interrogativas: Creating and answering questions (Textbook p. 70)

02-19 ¿Cómo es la vida de Mario? Look at the images below and then complete the answers to the questions about Mario's life at school as in the model. To avoid being redundant, omit the known subject (*Mario*).

9:00 A.M., Sala de clase

1:00 P.M.–1:30 P.M., El jardín de la universidad con los amigos

10:00 A.M.–12:00 P.M., Trabajo en el centro de tutores

6:30 P.M., Autobús a su casa

12:00 P.M.–1:00 P.M., Cafetería

8:00 P.M., Preparación para dos exámenes

Nombre: ______________________ Fecha: ______________________

1. ¿A qué hora tiene clase?

Tiene clase a las nueve.

2. ¿Cuántas horas trabaja?

Trabaja dos horas.

3. ¿Dónde come?

Come en la Cafeteria.

4. ¿Con quiénes habla después de (*after*) sus clases?

Habla con sus amigos después de sus clases.

5. ¿Adónde regresa a las seis y media?

Regresa a su casa a las seis y media.

6. ¿Por qué tiene que (*has to*) estudiar?

Tiene que estudiar porque tiene dos examenes mañana.

02-20 Tus hábitos y costumbres

Paso 1. Respond to the following questions about your habits and your life at school using complete sentences like those in the model. Notice that, in order to avoid being redundant, you should not use the subject pronoun **yo** in your responses.

MODELO ¿Tomas apuntes en clase todos los días?
Sí, tomo apuntes en clase todos los días. OR *No, no tomo apuntes en clase todos los días.*

1. ¿Trabajas más de (*more than*) cinco horas a la semana?

No, no trabajo mas de cinco horas a la semana

2. ¿Estudias los sábados y/o los domingos?

Si, yo estudio los sabados y los domingos

3. ¿Durante cuántas horas lees y estudias todas las semanas?

Leo y estudio diez durante todas las semanas

4. ¿Escribes muchos apuntes cuando lees?

Si, escribo muchos apuntes cuando leo

5. ¿Recibes muchos e-mails de tus amigos?

No, no recibo muchos e-mails de mis amigos

Nombre: ______________________ Fecha: ______________________

Vocabulario

5. Los números 100–1.000: Counting from 100–1,000 (Textbook p. 72)

02-24 ¿Cuál es el precio? Listen to each price and match each object with its most accurate price.

1. ______________ a. un iPad de Mac
2. ______________ b. el libro para la clase de español
3. ______________ c. un disco compacto
4. ______________ d. un televisor con una pantalla plana (*flat screen*) LCD de 46 pulgadas (*inches*)
5. ______________ e. un teléfono móvil con cámara digital y con reproductor (*player*) mp3

02-25 Datos importantes. Listen as Clara tells her supervisor at the university bookstore about their next order. Help them by writing down the number of each item they need to buy. Use numerals, not words, to write you answers.

1. cuadernos ______________
2. computadoras portátiles (*portable*) ______________
3. calculadoras científicas ______________
4. libros para la clase de biología 101 ______________
5. libros para la clase de español 101 ______________
6. diccionarios ______________

02-26 Los estudiantes internacionales. Susana works at the International Center of her university and shares with you some statistics about the number of international students enrolled this year. Listen and write the number of students from each country who are studying at her institution.

1. China ______________
2. Taiwan ______________
3. Hong Kong ______________
4. Japón ______________
5. México ______________
6. Canadá ______________

02-27 Heritage Language: *tu español*. It can be difficult to remember how to correctly say numbers in Spanish, especially course numbers. Because we spend most of our time talking about university studies in English, it is easy to think of course numbers in English and it may feel awkward to say them in Spanish.

Paso 1. Here is Olga's schedule for this semester. Choose three of her classes in order to practice saying what courses she is taking, when they take place and where they take place. Remember to use the correct conjugation of **tener** and to use **los** to state on which days of the week each class takes place, **a las** or **a la** to indicate the time and **en** to indicate the location.

MODELO Olga tiene la clase de japonés ciento uno, "Lengua japonesa, nivel elemental", los lunes, los miércoles y los viernes a las nueve menos cuarto de la mañana en la sala ciento diez del Centro de Idiomas.

El horario de Olga

lunes, miércoles y viernes

8:45 Japonés 101: Lengua japonesa, nivel elemental (Sala 110, Centro de Idiomas)

10:00 Matemáticas 114: Introducción al cálculo y la geometría analítica (Sala 214, Edificio Central)

11:00 Español 570: La novela hispanoamericana de los años 60 (Sala 245, Facultad de Filosofía y Letras)

1:00 Psicología 350: Introducción a la psicología cognitiva (Sala 347, Facultad de Ciencias Sociales)

martes y jueves

10:00 Arte 270: El muralismo mexicano y chicano en su contexto histórico y social (Sala 115, Facultad de Filosofía y Letras)

12:30 Música 410: Música afro-cubana (Auditorio Central, Teatro Bebo Valdés)

Paso 2. Now write down your own schedule, indicating when and where each class takes place.

____

____

____

____

____

____

____

Paso 3. Now use your notes above to describe at least three classes from your own schedule. Remember to use the correct conjugation of **tener** and to use **los** to state on which days of the week each class takes place, **a las** or **a la** to indicate the time and **en** to indicate the location.

Nombre: ______________________ Fecha: ______________________

02-30 Las cosas que tenemos. Your new friend Diego is interested in learning more about students in the United States. Listen to his questions and then write your answers in complete sentences below. Be sure to follow the model closely; you should avoid unnecessary repetition by not using subjects or subject pronouns in your responses.

1. ______________________.
2. ______________________.
3. ______________________.
4. ______________________.
5. ______________________.

02-31 ¿Qué tienen tú y tus amigos?

Paso 1. Categorize the words in the word bank according to the person who has the following items: you, one of your two friends, both of your friends, or both of your friends as well as you.

un teléfono móvil	una computadora	un televisor
unos DVDs	una radio	un/a compañero/a de cuarto
dos compañeros/as de cuarto	un reproductor mp3	muchos discos compactos

1. Yo: ______________________
2. Amigo 1: ______________________
3. Amigo 2: ______________________
4. Mis amigos 1 y 2: ______________________
5. Mis amigos y yo: ______________________

Paso 2. Use your notes above to describe what you and your friends have. Be careful to use **tengo** when discussing the item that only you have, **tiene** when discussing items that only one of your friends have, **tienen** when discussing items that your friends have and that you do not, and **tenemos** for items that you and at least one of your friends both have.

Paso 3. Now write a short paragraph comparing and contrasting what you and your friends have. Be careful to use the correct forms of the verb **tener** throughout.

____

____

____

____

____

____

____

____

02-32 Heritage Language: *tu español*. Cognates can be extremely helpful when one is trying to communicate in another language. However, false cognates can create confusion and misunderstandings. For that reason, it is wise to keep track of these words.

Paso 1. Indicate if each word is a cognate or a false cognate.

1. residencia — cognado — falso cognado
2. laboratorio — cognado — falso cognado
3. dormitorio — cognado — falso cognado
4. librería — cognado — falso cognado
5. apartamento — cognado — falso cognado
6. computadora — cognado — falso cognado

Paso 2. Select the correct meaning of each word.

7. residencia
   a. residence
   b. dorm
8. laboratorio
   a. classroom
   b. laboratory
9. dormitorio
   a. dorm
   b. bedroom
10. librería
    a. bookstore
    b. library
11. apartamento
    a. apartment
    b. bedroom
12. computadora
    a. calculator
    b. computer

Nombre: ______________________ Fecha: ______________________

02-45 Nuestras preferencias.

Paso 1. Take a moment to think about yourself and one person who is close to you. Consider what each of your favorite things and activities are. Jot down as many ideas in Spanish as possible, without repeating anything.

Yo

1. Me gusta:

____

____

2. Me gustan:

____

____

Una persona importante para mí

3. Le gusta:

____

____

4. Le gustan:

____

____

Paso 2. Now practice describing your likes, being careful to use the correct form of the verb **gustar** in your responses.

Nombre: ______________________ Fecha: ______________________

02-46 Heritage Language: *tu español.*

Paso 1. While the term **gustar** is the most common term used to express likes and dislikes across the entire Spanish-speaking world, in some regions and countries, other terms are also used. The following verbs are also conjugated the same way as **gustar** and are all used to express very strong, positive feelings and opinions. Complete each sentence with the correct conjugation of the verb in parentheses.

1. Me ______________ (chiflar) la música mexicana.
2. Le ______________ (encantar) todas sus clases.
3. Nos ______________ (ilusionar) estudiar en México.
4. Les ______________ (entusiasmar) las excursiones a las ruinas de los mayas.
5. Me ______________ (fascinar) el arte de Frida Kahlo.

Paso 2. In Spanish many other verbs work just like **gustar.** The following verbs should look very familiar to you because of their similarity to the adjectives for emotions and states of being that you have learned. Complete each sentence with the correct form of the verb provided, paying attention to the way it is conjugated. You may use each verb only once.

cansa	aburre	enojan	preocupan

6. Estoy nervioso porque necesito estudiar mucho y aprender bien la materia para dos exámenes que tengo hoy.

   Los exámenes me ______________.

7. Le gusta mucho ir al gimnasio para hacer mucho ejercicio durante dos horas todos los días. Hacer tanto (*so much*) ejercicio le ______________.

8. La clase que no es interesante nos ______________.

9. Cuando trabajo mucho en los proyectos y no recibo buenas notas, las malas notas (D's y F's) me

   ______________.

Vocabulario

10. Los deportes y los pasatiempos: Offering opinions on sports and pastimes (Textbook p. 81)

02-47 ¿Qué le gusta? Look at the names of the following famous people and the list of things or activities that they might like. Using expressions with the verb **gustar** along with the expressions provided, create logical sentences about these people.

el básquetbol	jugar al fútbol	~~jugar al golf~~	los bailes y la música	jugar al béisbol
las bicicletas	jugar al fútbol americano	las novelas	jugar al tenis	

1.  A Pau Gasol ____.

2.  A Shakira ____.

3.  A Leo Messi ____.

4. A Miguel Indurain ____.

5. A Gabriel García Márquez ____.

6. A Albert Pujols ____.

7. A Rafael Nadal ____.

Nombre: ______________________ Fecha: ______________________

02-48 ¿Preguntas lógicas o preguntas ilógicas? Listen to each question and indicate if it is a **pregunta lógica** (*logical question*) or if it is a **pregunta ilógica** (*illogical question*).

1. pregunta lógica pregunta ilógica
2. pregunta lógica pregunta ilógica
3. pregunta lógica pregunta ilógica
4. pregunta lógica pregunta ilógica
5. pregunta lógica pregunta ilógica
6. pregunta lógica pregunta ilógica

02-49 ¿Qué, cuándo, con quién, y dónde?

Paso 1. List five activities that you particularly like doing, in Spanish. For each one indicate also when you like doing those things, with whom you like doing them and where you like doing them.

	Actividad	Mes / Estación	Persona(s)	Lugar
1.				
2.				
3.				
4.				
5.				

Paso 2. Using the information that you organized in **Paso 1,** describe at least three of your favorite pastimes, when and where you generally do them and with whom you like to do them.

Paso 3. Using the information that you organized in **Paso 1** and that you described in Paso 2, construct a short paragraph describing your favorite pastimes, when you like doing those activities, with whom you like doing them, and where you enjoy doing them. You may find words like **también, y,** and **pero** useful as you try to connect your ideas.

____

____

____

____

____

____

____

02-50 Heritage Language: *tu español*. Although the sports and pastimes you have learned about are known throughout much of the Spanish-speaking world, there are also many other activities that are popular in Spanish-speaking countries. For each activity, indicate if it is an indoor activity or an outdoor activity. If necessary, use the Appendix 3 *También se dice* section of your textbook or the Internet to find out what the sport or activity is.

1. el senderismo indoor outdoor either
2. el alpinismo indoor outdoor either
3. el ráquetbol indoor outdoor either
4. la pesca indoor outdoor either
5. el jai alai indoor outdoor either

Nota cultural: Los deportes en el mundo hispano (Textbook p. 84)

02-51 Sports and pastimes in the Spanish-speaking world. Choose the correct response or responses to the following questions about sports and pastimes in the Spanish-speaking world.

1. ¿Cuál es el deporte nacional de muchos países del mundo hispánico?

   _____ el básquetbol

   _____ el fútbol

   _____ el béisbol

   _____ el atletismo

2. ¿Cuáles son otros deportes populares en el mundo hispánico?

   _____ el básquetbol

   _____ el fútbol americano

   _____ el tenis

   _____ el béisbol

3. ¿Cuáles de los siguientes países participan en los Juegos Panamericanos?

   _____ Cuba

   _____ España

   _____ Argentina

   _____ México

4. ¿Cuándo tienen lugar (*take place*) los Juegos Panamericanos?

   _____ el mismo año que los Juegos Olímpicos

   _____ un año antes de los Juegos Olímpicos

   _____ cada cuatro años

   _____ un año después de los Juegos Olímpicos

5. ¿Cuáles son algunos deportes que ofrecen (*they offer*) en la UNAM?

   _____ béisbol

   _____ vóleibol

   _____ fútbol americano

   _____ judo

   _____ golf

   _____ natación

Nombre: ______________________ Fecha: ______________________

Escucha (Textbook p. 86)

02-52 En la librería.

Paso 1

1. Listen as Merche and Amaya converse about work and classes, and select the words that you hear in their conversation.

______ bolígrafos	______ cuaderno
______ trabajo	______ ciencias
______ libros	______ idiomas
______ clases	______ compañeros
______ lápices	______ mochila
______ dinero	______ dólares

Paso 2. Listen again and indicate whether the following statements are **Cierto** or **Falso.**

2. Amaya trabaja en una cafetería.	Cierto	Falso
3. Merche necesita comprar cuadernos y bolígrafos.	Cierto	Falso
4. Amaya trabaja 10 horas a la semana.	Cierto	Falso
5. Merche necesita una nueva mochila.	Cierto	Falso
6. Merche toma seis clases en total.	Cierto	Falso
7. El precio total es $367.00.	Cierto	Falso

Paso 3. Listen to the conversation between Amaya and Merche once more in order to relate what really happened in the bookstore. This time, rewrite the selected portions of the statements that are false in order to make them true. For those that are true, leave the statement as it is.

8. Amaya trabaja en una <u>cafetería.</u>
9. Merche necesita comprar <u>cuadernos y bolígrafos</u>.
10. Amaya trabaja <u>10</u> horas a la semana.
11. Merche necesita una nueva <u>mochila</u>.
12. Merche toma <u>seis</u> clases en total.
13. El precio total es <u>$367.00</u>.

02-53 La idea general. Listen to the conversation between Merche and Amaya and, using one sentence in English, relay the gist of it.

____

____

¡Conversemos! (Textbook p. 86)

02-54 Mi universidad. You are working at the Office of International Education at your campus. One of your responsibilities is to help international students adjust to life at your school by conducting orientation sessions and holding individual and group meetings. Today you are meeting with a student from Mexico. Help him by answering his questions.

1. ¿Qué especialidades crees que son muy difíciles en esta universidad?
2. ¿Qué especialidades crees que son fáciles?
3. ¿Cuál es tu especialidad y por qué te gusta?
4. ¿Qué profesores y clases crees que son interesantes?
5. ¿Qué profesores y clases crees que son aburridos?
6. ¿Qué actividades extracurriculares te gustan? ¿Por qué? ¿Cuáles no te gustan? ¿Por qué no?

Nombre: ______________________ Fecha: ______________________

Escribe (Textbook p. 87)

02-55 Tu mejor amigo/a y tú.

Paso 1. Provide the following basic information about yourself and your best friend; also indicate any information that is common to you both.

1. Características físicas

____

____

____

2. Personalidad

____

____

____

3. Universidad

____

____

____

4. Especialidad

____

____

____

5. Pasatiempos

____

____

____

6. Deportes favoritos

____

____

____

Paso 2. Using the information you provided in Paso 1, describe yourself and your best friend. Before speaking, take a moment to quickly review the information about verb forms in **Capítulos 1–2** (especially the **yo** forms, the **él** or **ella** forms, and the **nosotros** forms of **ser, tener**, regular **–ar, –er,** and **–ir** verbs; and forms of **gustar** that you have learned).

Paso 3. Un programa de televisión. You and your best friend are entering a competition to be part of a new reality show. As part of your application, you need to write a general description of yourselves. Before writing, review once again the information about verb forms in **Capítulos 1–2.** Then, use the information in **Paso 1** to write your description. Finally, review your work to ensure that your adjectives correspond to the gender of the person to whom you are referring and that you have used the correct verb forms.

____

____

____

____

____

____

____

____

____

____

Nombre: ______________________________ Fecha: ______________________

Cultura: México (Textbook pp. 88–89)

02-56 ¡Qué interesante es México! Based on what you learned about Mexico in **Capítulo 2,** choose the correct answers to the following questions.

1. Las universidades mexicanas normalmente no tienen ______________.
   a. gimnasios
   b. residencias estudiantiles
   c. muchos estudiantes
   d. estadios
   e. piscinas

2. La UNAM está en ______________ .
   a. Oaxaca
   b. Tepotzlán
   c. Ciudad de México
   d. Morelia
   e. Guadalajara

3. La UNAM es ______________ .
   a. la primera universidad de América Latina
   b. la universidad más importante de América Latina
   c. la universidad más pequeña de América Latina
   d. la universidad más moderna de América Latina
   e. la universidad más grande de América Latina

4. El equipo de fútbol de la UNAM se llama ______________ .
   a. los Pumas
   b. los Jaguares
   c. los Tigres
   d. los Gatos
   e. los Leopardos

5. La ciudad de Oaxaca es famosa porque tiene ______________ .
   a. una universidad muy grande
   b. muchos artesanos
   c. un equipo de fútbol importante
   d. muchos estudiantes
   e. los Juegos Panamericanos

6. Frida Kahlo es ______________ .
   a. una pintora famosa por sus murales de temas históricos y sociales
   b. una artesana famosa por su hojalatería
   c. una artesana famosa por su cestería
   d. una pintora famosa por sus autorretratos psicológicos
   e. una artesana famosa por su cerámica

Nombre: ______________________ Fecha: ______________________

02-57 Vistas culturales: México. View the video segments in order to complete each part of the activity. You will likely not understand all of the words that you hear, but you should relax because you are capable of understanding more than enough to be able to respond to the questions without difficulty.

México: Introducción. Read the questions, then watch the video and complete each sentence with the correct information.

1. La capital de México es ______________________.

2. La población de México es ______________________.

México: Geografía. Read the questions, then watch the video and select the correct response or responses to each question.

3. México es aproximadamente 3 veces el tamaño (*three times the size*) de

   ______ los Estados Unidos

   ______ Texas

   ______ Guatemala

   ______ Arizona

4. México tiene frontera con

   ______ los Estados Unidos

   ______ El Salvador

   ______ Nicaragua

   ______ Guatemala

5. México tiene costas con

   ______ el oceáno Pacífico

   ______ el mar Mediterráneo

   ______ el golfo de México

Nombre: ______________________________ Fecha: ______________________

México: Presencia indígena. Read the questions, then watch the video and select with which indigenous group of Mexico each place or item is associated.

6. San Lorenzo
   a. los olmecas
   b. los toltecas
   c. los mayas
   d. los aztecas

7. Laguna de los Cerros
   a. los olmecas
   b. los toltecas
   c. los mayas
   d. los aztecas

8. juegos similares al básquetbol
   a. los olmecas
   b. los toltecas
   c. los mayas
   d. los aztecas

9. Teotihuacán
   a. los olmecas
   b. los toltecas
   c. los mayas
   d. los aztecas

10. El templo de Quetzalcóatl
   a. los olmecas
   b. los toltecas
   c. los mayas
   d. los aztecas

11. La pirámide del sol
   a. los olmecas
   b. los toltecas
   c. los mayas
   d. los aztecas

12. El calendario más exacto del mundo
   a. los olmecas
   b. los toltecas
   c. los mayas
   d. los aztecas

13. La astronomía
   a. los olmecas
   b. los toltecas
   c. los mayas
   d. los aztecas

14. Uxmal
   a. los olmecas
   b. los toltecas
   c. los mayas
   d. los aztecas

15. Aztlán
   a. los olmecas
   b. los toltecas
   c. los mayas
   d. los aztecas

16. Tenochtitlán
   a. los olmecas
   b. los toltecas
   c. los mayas
   d. los aztecas

Más cultura

02-58 Las universidades en el mundo hispánico.

Read the following information about some of the characteristics of universities and university systems in many Spanish-speaking countries, and then answer the questions that follow.

- En el mundo hispano, el proceso de admisión a las universidades varía (*varies*) en diferentes países. En unos países, todos los estudiantes en el país toman un examen. Después, las notas (*grades*) de los estudiantes determinan su futuro académico. Para un estudiante con una nota muy buena, normalmente es posible estudiar su especialidad preferida en su universidad favorita. Un estudiante que tiene una nota muy mala no tiene muchas opciones —es posible estudiar una especialidad, pero no necesariamente su especialidad preferida en su universidad preferida.

- El proceso de admisión también varía dentro de los países y también, a veces, dentro de las universidades. En unas universidades, es necesario completar un examen de admisión y hacer entrevistas (*interviews*) de admisión. En unas facultades también es necesario presentar más de un examen para poder (*to be able to*) estudiar una de sus especialidades.

- Los exámenes de admisión a las universidades en el mundo hispánico no son exactamente como los exámenes que muchos estudiantes de los Estados Unidos toman. Aunque (*although*) tienen partes similares para evaluar las habilidades de los estudiantes para hacer las matemáticas, para comprender vocabulario y para leer, muchos exámenes también tienen secciones donde los estudiantes tienen que contestar preguntas sobre historia, literatura, y política internacional.

- Dentro de las universidades, las notas en muchos lugares del mundo hispánico se basan en un sistema de cero a diez. En estos lugares, para aprobar (*pass*) una clase es necesario tener un cinco. Si un estudiante tiene un nueve o un diez, está muy feliz porque no es común recibir notas muy altas. Es más común recibir un seis, un siete y, si estudias mucho, un ocho. También es muy común para muchos estudiantes no aprobar todas las clases todos los semestres. Ellos no tienen que tomar la clase otra vez (*again*) si no lo desean (*if they do not want to*); solamente tienen que tomar y aprobar el examen final de la clase.

1. In general, how does the university admissions process in Spanish-speaking countries compare to the process that you underwent when you applied to your school(s)?

____

____

____

____

2. How do admissions exams in the Spanish-speaking countries compare to standardized tests required by many schools in the United States?

____

____

____

____

3. How does the grading system described above compare to the one that is used at your university? How common is it for students to receive the highest possible grade in your system? How common is it for students to fail one or two courses every semester?

____

____

____

____

Nombre: ______________________________ Fecha: ______________________

02-59 Heritage Language: *tu mundo hispano*. Investigate the similarities and differences between your university and a university in a Spanish-speaking country. Select a university located in a city and country where you would enjoy studying for a semester or for an academic year. Your campus Study Abroad Office or Office of International Education can help and might even put you in contact with an exchange student who can give you firsthand information about his or her home university.

Paso 1. Use the following questions to guide your comparative research about your university and the university you have chosen to learn about.

¿Cómo se llama (*What is the name of*) la universidad y dónde está?

1. Mi universidad: ____________________
2. Una universidad hispana: ____________________

¿Aproximadamente cuántos estudiantes hay en la universidad?

3. Mi universidad: ____________________
4. Una universidad hispana: ____________________

¿Cuántas facultades (*colleges* or *schools*) tiene la universidad?

5. Mi universidad: ____________________
6. Una universidad hispana: ____________________

¿Cómo se llama el departamento de tu especialidad y en qué facultad está? Si la universidad hispana no tiene tu especialidad, ¿qué especialidades tiene que te gustan? ¿En qué facultad(es) están?

7. Mi universidad: ____________________
8. Una universidad hispana: ____________________

¿En qué tipo de actividades extracurriculares participan los estudiantes? ¿Tiene equipos importantes de algún deporte? Si sí, ¿cuál(es)?

9. Mi universidad: ____________________
10. Una universidad hispana: ____________________

Paso 2. Using your responses in **Paso 1,** briefly describe how your own university compares to the university you have researched. Be careful to use the correct forms of the verbs **tener, estar, necesitar,** and **participar** in your responses.

Nombre: ______________________________ Fecha: ________________________

Ambiciones siniestras

Episodio 2

Lectura: *Las solicitudes* (Textbook p. 90)

02-60 Los personajes. Based on what you have read in your text from *Ambiciones siniestras*, indicate which character or characters would logically make each statement below.

1. Mis padres son divorciados.	Alejandra	Manolo	Cisco
2. Soy un/a estudiante muy bueno/a.	Alejandra	Manolo	Cisco
3. Me gusta el arte.	Alejandra	Manolo	Cisco
4. Me gustan las computadoras.	Alejandra	Manolo	Cisco
5. Deseo estudiar medicina.	Alejandra	Manolo	Cisco
6. Soy una persona muy creativa.	Alejandra	Manolo	Cisco
7. Hablo español.	Alejandra	Manolo	Cisco

Video: *La aventura comienza* (Textbook p. 92)

02-61 Otros personajes. Read the following statements. Then, as you view the video, indicate which character or characters would logically make each statement.

1. Soy de Nueva York.	Marisol	Lupe	Eduardo
2. Me gusta el periodismo.	Marisol	Lupe	Eduardo
3. Creo que la historia es interesante.	Marisol	Lupe	Eduardo
4. Estoy en mi tercer año de la universidad.	Marisol	Lupe	Eduardo
5. Me gustan los deportes.	Marisol	Lupe	Eduardo
6. Me gustan las novelas policíacas.	Marisol	Lupe	Eduardo
7. Trabajo como voluntario/a con niños.	Marisol	Lupe	Eduardo
8. Hablo más de dos idiomas.	Marisol	Lupe	Eduardo

Nombre: ______________________________ Fecha: ______________________

02-62 Marisol, Lupe y Eduardo. View the video again in order to extract more detailed information about the characters.

Paso 1. Complete the following statements with information that you learn about the characters in the video. If necessary, view the episode more than once.

1. El nombre completo de Marisol es: Marisol Soledad Valenzuela [López, Calle, Salme].
2. El nombre completo de Lupe es: Guadalupe Iriarte [Chacón, Chávez, Girón].
3. El nombre completo de Eduardo es: Eduardo Caña [Rodríguez, Suarez, Jiménez].
4. La especialidad de Marisol es [sociología, psicología, ingeniería].

Paso 2. Complete the following statements about the characters.

5. Las aficiones de Eduardo son: jugar al ________________ y ________________.
6. Marisol ________________ como voluntaria en el hospital.
7. Eduardo trabaja como voluntario en una organización para los ________________ de su área.
8. A Eduardo le gusta pasar tiempo con su ________________.

Nombre: ______________________ Fecha: ______________________

02-63 Conexiones y conclusiones

Paso 1. Personas similares. View the video one more time. Then, using complete sentences in Spanish, answer the following questions about the characters.

1. ¿Qué tienen en común (*in common*) Lupe y Eduardo?

____

2. ¿Qué tienen en común Marisol y Eduardo?

____

3. ¿Qué tienen en común Lupe, Marisol y Eduardo?

____

4. ¿Qué tienes tú en común con Lupe, Marisol y Eduardo?

____

5. ¿Por qué cree el Sr. Verdugo que Marisol, Lupe y Eduardo "son perfectos"? Escribe por lo menos (*at least*) tres adjetivos que él usa en su descripción de los chicos.

____

Paso 2. Tus conclusiones. Answer the questions about the conclusion of this episode using English or Spanish.

6. What kind of assumption does Sr. Verdugo make about the three students' language skills based on the fact that "**todos tienen nombres hispanos**"? Do you think this assumption is common? Do you think it is wise? Why or why not?

____

____

____

____

____

____

7. Finally, considering the adjectives that Sr. Verdugo used to describe these three characters and the fact that he mentions that he hopes they like "**dinero,**" hypothesize about what kind of e-mail message you think he sent to them. Be creative!

____

____

____

____

____

____

Comunidades

02-64 Experiential learning: Compras en línea. Visit the online shopping site of a Mexican retailer, such as **Cimaco**. Investigate the prices of at least ten common back-to-school items that many college students buy. Then find the current exchange rate for the Mexican peso and convert each price to U.S. dollars. Describe how the prices compare to what you would pay for such items in the United States. Take the findings of your research to class in order to compare your results with those of your classmates. In groups, relate to each other in Spanish which products you found and what their prices are.

02-65 Service learning: Estudiantes hispanohablantes.

Paso 1. Obtain an electronic copy of your campus map and request permission to create a bilingual version of it to be used by Spanish-speaking visitors and current and future students. Work with your class to label all of the buildings that have specific functions in Spanish, while also leaving the English words visible. For example, where the map shows the campus post office, you should write **Oficina de Correos** and for the dining hall you should write **Cafetería.** Submit the final bilingual map to the Office of Admission or Recruitment as a gift from your Spanish class.

Paso 2. Studying in another country far away from home is an exciting and extremely rewarding experience, and a fabulous opportunity for personal and academic growth. Spending time with international students on your own campus and talking with them about their experiences and perspectives can be just as valuable an experience for you, and at the same time you can make another person feel more welcome in your campus community. Contact your university's Office of International Relations and volunteer to serve as a buddy or mentor for an international student. Let them know that you are studying Spanish and that, ideally, you would like to help a Spanish-speaking exchange student.

Nombre: ______________________ Fecha: ______________________

- **Otras características importantes de tu casa**

11. ______________________

Paso 2. Now using the information above, write a short paragraph describing your dream house.

12. ______________________

03-06 Mi casa ideal. Without looking at your notes or your textbook, describe orally your own personal ideal home. Is it modern, traditional, or rustic? Is it large and luxurious, or is it small and quaint?

03-07 Heritage Language: *tu español*. While cognates make it easier to communicate in another language, it is important to keep in mind that not all words that look alike actually correspond perfectly in meaning. In order to avoid confusing the following words, write down the correct meaning of each word. Some of the words are new, so you may have to look them up in a dictionary.

1. **dormitorio** / dormitory

____

____

2. **jardín** / garden

____

____

3. **patio** / patio

____

____

4. **salón** / salon / saloon

____

____

____

Nombre: ______________________ Fecha: ______________________

Belén y sus amigos

querer	salir	poder	decir	ser	oír	hacer	estar

Al contrario, mi hermana y sus amigos (7) ______________ muy irresponsables y un poco locos (*crazy*). Belén (8) ______________ con sus amigos a conciertos y discotecas todas las noches. Ellos no (9) ______________ estudiar y no (10) ______________ su tarea nunca. Cuando Belén (11) ______________ en sus clases, no (12) ______________ tomar buenos apuntes; a causa de (*due to*) su reproductor de mp3, ella no (13) ______________ qué (14) ______________ sus profesores.

03-18 Heritage Langage: *tu español.* When speaking Spanish, many people pronounce the **s** in some words very lightly, especially when it appears at the end of the word. As a result, some people forget to include the **s** in their writing. Listen to the following conversation between two students and use the context to determine which of the two verb endings is appropriate for the message they are communicating.

1. ¿[Puedes, Puede] hablar?
2. [Estás, Está] muy contento …
3. De domingo a jueves [estudias, estudia] mucho.
4. … todos los viernes y sábados [sales, sale] …
5. ¿También [haces, hace] esas cosas?
6. ¿[Tienes, Tiene] planes para este fin de semana?
7. ¿[Quieres, Quiere] salir conmigo?
8. [Eres, Es] tan simpático.

Nota cultural: ¿Dónde viven los españoles? (Textbook p. 105)

03-19 Las viviendas en España. Complete each statement with the correct information from your textbook.

MODELO La capital de España es *Madrid*.

1. ______________ es una ciudad grande que está en el noreste de España.
2. Como en Nueva York, la vida en Madrid y Barcelona es ______________ y ______________.
3. El costo de la vida en la ciudad es muy ______________.
4. Muchas personas que no viven en la ciudad tienen la ______________ cerca de su casa.
5. Algunas de las casas en los pueblos pequeños en España son ______________ y tienen ______________.
6. Muchas personas en el campo trabajan en la ______________.
7. En comparación con la vida en la ciudad, la vida en muchos pueblos pequeños y en el campo es más ______________.

Vocabulario

3. Los muebles y otros objetos de la casa: Elaborating on rooms (Textbook p. 106)

03-20 ¿Dónde está? Associate each piece of furniture with the room in the house where you would most logically find it. Be sure to use each room only once.

1. el inodoro ______	a. la sala
2. la cama ______	b. el comedor
3. el sofá ______	c. la oficina
4. la estufa ______	d. el dormitorio
5. la mesa ______	e. el baño
6. el estante de libros ______	f. la cocina

03-21 ¿Lógico o ilógico? Read the sentences and indicate if they are logical (**lógico**) or illogical (**ilógico**).

1. Tenemos una alfombra en el comedor. lógico ilógico
2. Tengo un bidet en el jardín. lógico ilógico
3. Tienen una colcha en la cocina. lógico ilógico
4. Tengo dos almohadas en mi dormitorio. lógico ilógico
5. Tengo un sillón en mi estante de libros. lógico ilógico
6. Tienes una ducha en tu armario. lógico ilógico
7. Tenemos un microondas en la cocina. lógico ilógico
8. Tenemos unos tocadores en la sala. lógico ilógico

03-22 ¿Es un buen precio? A friend of yours is shopping online and is unsure about whether or not the prices are reasonable. For each question, indicate if the price is **caro** (*expensive*), **razonable** (*reasonable*), or **barato** (*inexpensive*).

1. $90 caro razonable barato
2. $900 caro razonable barato
3. $570 caro razonable barato
4. $2 caro razonable barato
5. $170 caro razonable barato
6. $77 caro razonable barato

Nombre: ______________________________ Fecha: ______________________________

03-23 Crucigrama. Complete the crossword puzzle with the correct household items.

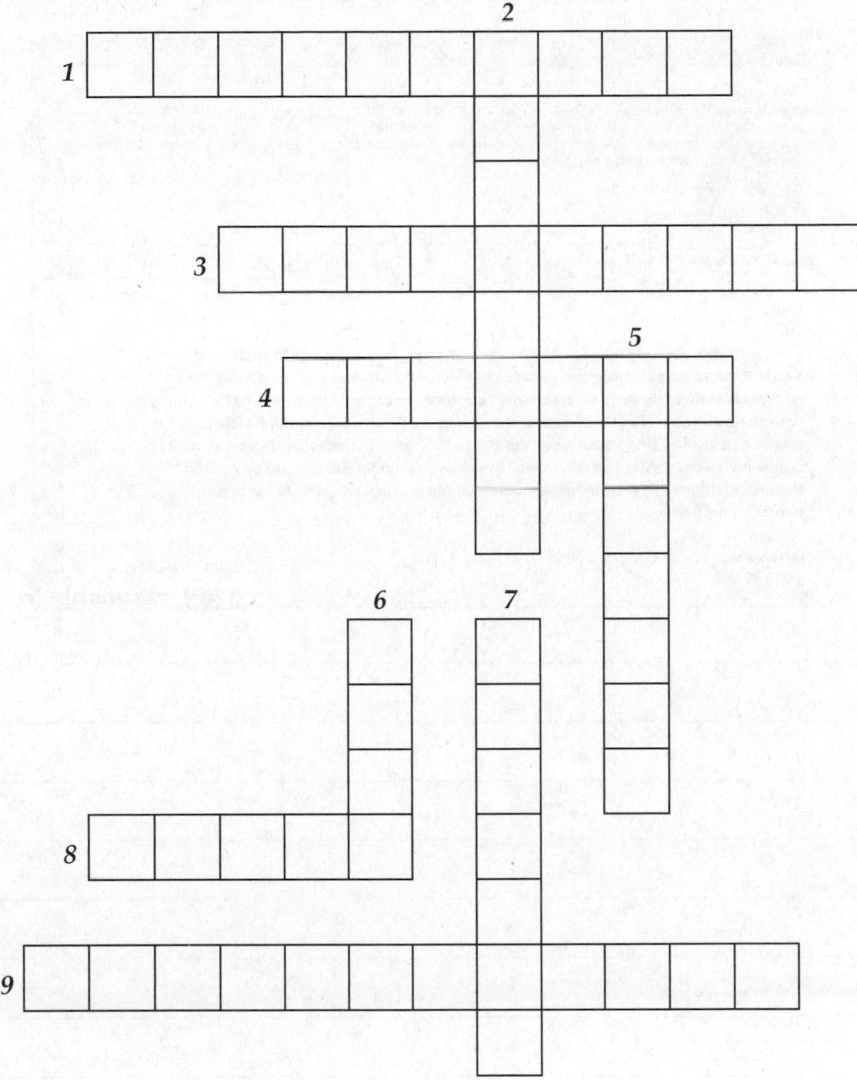

1. con este aparato (*equipment; machine*), es mucho más fácil limpiar los platos después de una comida (*meal*)
2. tengo una en mi cama y la uso todas las noches para dormir bien
3. con este aparato, es muy fácil calentar (*warm up*) comida muy rápidamente
4. este es el mueble donde pongo mis libros
5. este es el mueble donde pongo mi ropa
6. este mueble está en mi dormitorio y lo uso para dormir (*to sleep*)
7. es necesario usar este aparato si quieres leer por la noche
8. esto está sobre (*on top of*) mi cama durante el invierno porque es muy necesaria cuando hace frío
9. este aparato mantiene (*maintains, keeps*) la comida fresca (*fresh*) durante más tiempo

Nombre: ______________________ Fecha: ______________________

03-24 ¿Qué necesito? You are mentoring a new student who is from Spain. She sent you the following e-mail to inquire about the supplies she may need. Read the message and then respond to it, answering all of her questions.

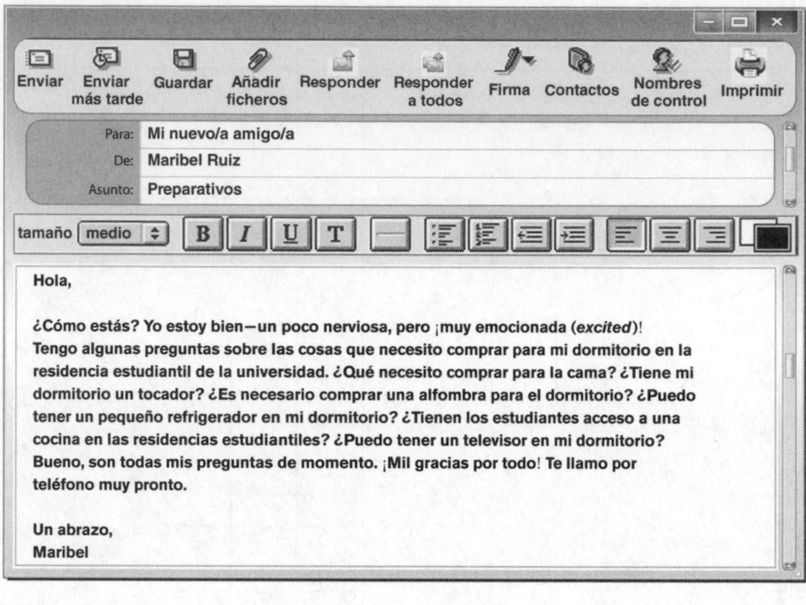

____

____

____

____

____

____

____

____

____

03-25 Heritage Language: *tu español*. Vocabulary often varies from one region to another in most languages; the Spanish language is especially rich with such variety. Match the following words with their synonyms. Before using a dictionary, try to figure out the meaning of the unfamiliar words by looking for similarities with other Spanish words that you have learned or for connections to English.

1. clóset ______	a. lavaplatos
2. librero ______	b. refrigerador
3. lavavajillas ______	c. estante de libros
4. váter (o wáter) ______	d. armario
5. frigorífico ______	e. inodoro
6. habitación ______	f. dormitorio

Nombre: ______________________ Fecha: ______________________

Comunicación II

Vocabulario

4. Los quehaceres de la casa: Sharing information about household chores (Textbook p. 109)

03-26 ¿Quién hace qué? Look at the drawing and then indicate who is doing what by writing the name or names of the person or people.

1. ¿Quién prepara la comida? ______________
2. ¿Quiénes arreglan sus dormitorios? ______________, ______________ y ______________
3. ¿Quiénes hacen la cama? ______________ y ______________
4. ¿Quiénes ponen la mesa? ______________ y ______________
5. ¿Quiénes lavan los platos? ______________ y ______________
6. ¿Quiénes sacuden los muebles? ______________ y ______________
7. ¿Quiénes guardan los libros en el estante? ______________ y ______________
8. ¿Quién saca la basura? ______________
9. ¿Quién pasa la aspiradora? ______________

03-27 Las responsabilidades en casa. Listen to the conversation between Donato and Leticia about household chores and then indicate who is responsible for each chore.

1. sacudir los muebles	Donato	Leticia	Los dos
2. pasar la aspiradora	Donato	Leticia	Los dos
3. preparar la comida	Donato	Leticia	Los dos
4. lavar los platos	Donato	Leticia	Los dos
5. limpiar la mesa	Donato	Leticia	Los dos
6. poner el lavaplatos	Donato	Leticia	Los dos
7. limpiar la cocina	Donato	Leticia	Los dos
8. lavar las cosas que no pueden poner en el lavaplatos	Donato	Leticia	Los dos
9. sacar la basura	Donato	Leticia	Los dos
10. hacer el café por la mañana	Donato	Leticia	Los dos

03-28 ¿Eres una persona limpia, organizada y responsable? Pedro and his housemates are looking for another person to live in the house with them. They would like to live with a person that is clean, organized and responsible. You would like to live in their house. Listen to each question about your habits and preferences relating to household chores and respond honestly, using complete sentences and following the model.

MODELO ¿Ayudas a arreglar tu casa todas las semanas?
Sí, ayudo a arreglar mi casa todas las semanas. / No, no ayudo a arreglar mi casa todas las semanas.

03-29 Heritage Language: *tu español*. Practice spelling words containing letters that are easily confused or omitted in Spanish. Write each word or expression that you hear.

1. ______________________________
2. ______________________________
3. ______________________________
4. ______________________________
5. ______________________________

Nombre: ______________________ Fecha: ______________________

Vocabulario

5. Los colores: Illustrating objects using colors (Textbook p. 111)

03-30 ¿De qué color es? Match each object to the color with which it is most commonly associated.

1. la planta	rojo	negro	verde
2. el lápiz	amarillo	rosado	azul
3. la pizarra	morado	negro	beige
4. la sangría	negro	blanco	rojo
5. el café	marrón	blanco	verde
6. el papel	marrón	rosado	blanco

03-31 ¿Cómo es la casa? Verónica has found the ideal house for her family. Listen to her conversation with her husband about the house, and then complete the sentences with the correct colors. Use the correct form of the colors, in masculine or feminine, and in singular or plural.

1. El exterior es ______________.

2. Tiene ventanas ______________.
3. Las paredes de la cocina son ______________.
4. Tiene un lavaplatos ______________.
5. La estufa es ______________.
6. El baño del primer piso tiene muebles ______________.
7. El otro baño tiene paredes ______________.
8. El dormitorio más grande es ______________.
9. Las paredes del dormitorio más pequeño son ______________.
10. El color que Verónica prefiere para los dormitorios es ______________.

03-32 Color para la casa. You are an interior decorator and have new clients who would like to radically change the look of some of the rooms in their home. Look at the photographs of the dining room and living room of the house in which neutral colors predominate. Using the vocabulary you have learned in this chapter, describe your new, significantly more colorful vision for their rooms by indicating what colors you will add to the rooms and in what furniture and areas of the rooms the colors appear in your proposed makeover.

____

____

____

____

____

____

____

____

____

____

03-33 Heritage Language: *tu español*. The words that you have learned for colors are used and understood across the Spanish-speaking world. However in some areas people use other words to convey these concepts. For each color, identify its alternative expression. Before using a dictionary, try to figure out the meaning of the unfamiliar words by looking for similarities with Spanish words that you have learned or for connections to English.

1. naranja ______	a. morado
2. café ______	b. rojo
3. rosa ______	c. anaranjado
4. púrpura ______	d. marrón
5. granate ______	e. rosado

Nombre: ______________________ Fecha: ______________________

Vocabulario

7. Los números 1.000–100.000.000: Counting from 1,000 to 100,000,000 (Textbook p. 116)

03-38 ¿Cuál es el precio? Associate each house or piece of furniture with its most logical price.

1. Una casa de cuatro pisos, seis dormitorios, seis baños, con piscina y vistas al océano _____
2. Un condominio pequeño de 2 dormitorios y un baño _____
3. Una lámpara muy elegante y moderna _____
4. Un tocador de estilo rústico, importado de México _____
5. Un televisor de pantalla (*screen*) plana de plasma de 50 pulgadas (*inches*) _____
6. Una casa muy bonita de tres pisos, cuatro dormitorios, dos baños, una cocina moderna, una sala y un comedor, en una ciudad _____

a. ochocientos setenta y cinco dólares
b. quinientos mil dólares
c. un millón cuatrocientos mil dólares
d. tres mil dólares
e. ciento cincuenta mil dólares
f. trescientos dólares

03-39 Fechas importantes. Listen as Clara describes when some of our most important resources were invented; then write, using numerals, the year that she indicates for each item.

1. El automóvil ______________
2. El teléfono ______________
3. La computadora personal ______________
4. La computadora portátil ______________
5. Google ______________
6. Wikipedia ______________

03-40 Tus fechas importantes. Think of some of the important years in your life and in the lives of your family and friends. Give the year that you were born (**nací**) and the years that at least three important people in your life were born (**nació**).

MODELO *Yo nací en mil novecientos noventa.*
Mi mejor amigo nació en mil novecientos ochenta y nueve.
Mi madre nació en mil novecientos sesenta y dos.

Nombre: ______________________________ Fecha: ______________________

03-41 Casas interesantes. You would like to buy a house. Listen to the information about the different houses and then fill in the table with the basics about each house. Do not write out the words for each number, simply use the digits. Remember to use periods instead of commas when writing numbers over one thousand.

	Dormitorios	Baños	Pisos	Precio
Casa 1	3	2	1	
Casa 2		1	3	
Casa 3		1	1	
Casa 4			2	
Casa 5			3	

03-42 Heritage Language: *tu español*. Remembering how to correctly say and write numbers in Spanish, particularly high numbers, can be a challenge. Practice saying and writing high numbers by completing the following steps.

Paso 1. Conduct research on housing in a Hispanic city where members of your own family live or have lived or on a city that you might enjoy visiting in the future. Find two properties for sale that you like: one average-sized property and one particularly large or luxurious property. Write down the number of bedrooms and bathrooms each house has, list other rooms in the homes and describe why the homes appeal to you.

1. Casa / Apartamento 1

____

____

____

____

2. Casa / Apartamento 2

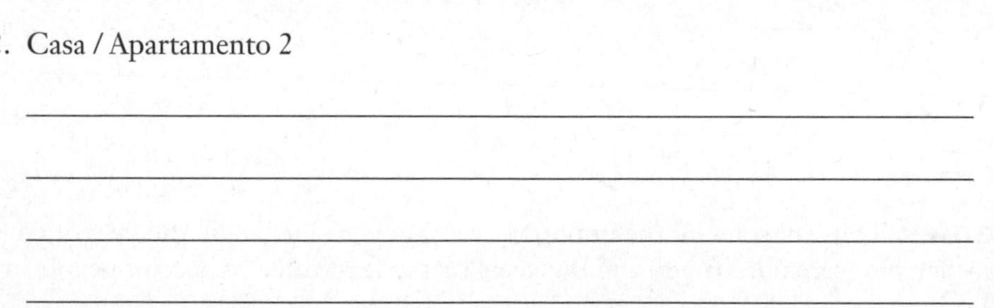

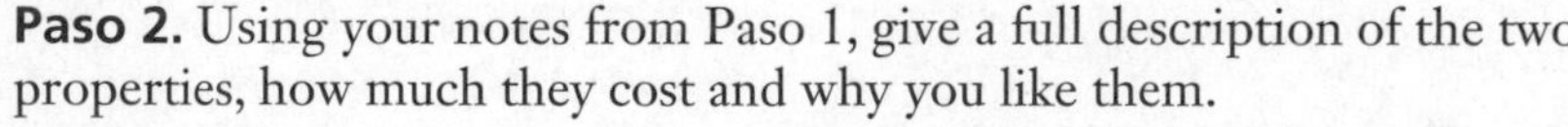

Paso 2. Using your notes from Paso 1, give a full description of the two properties, how much they cost and why you like them.

Nombre: ______________________ Fecha: ______________________

Gramática

8. Hay: Stating *There is / There are* (Textbook p. 119)

03-43 Características de las casas en venta. Answer the questions about the houses that are for sale. For the numbers, write out the words, as in the model.

Casa adosada	Chalet de lujo	Piso	Altillo	Estudio
120m², jardín de 100m², 4 hab., 2 b. 560.000 €	200m², jardín de 300m², piscina, 6 hab., 4 b, cocina moderna 1.570.000 €	60 m², 3 hab., 1 b., cocina nueva, suelos de parqué, semi-amueblado 427.000 €	150 m², terraza de 100 m², 2 balcones, 4 hab., 2 b., cocina amueblada 1.150.000 €	30 m², céntrico, cocina, 1 baño, 1 balcón 210.000 €

MODELO ¿Cuántos balcones hay en el altillo
dos

1. ¿Cuántas habitaciones hay en el piso? ______________.
2. ¿Cuántos baños hay en el estudio? ______________.
3. ¿Cuántas habitaciones hay en la casa adosada? ______________.
4. ¿Cuántos baños hay en el chalet de lujo? ______________.
5. ¿Hay una cocina nueva en el piso? ______________.
6. ¿Hay una cocina moderna en la casa adosada? ______________.

03-44 ¿Cuántos hay? Use the expression **hay** to answer the following questions. Use short but complete sentences, following the model.

MODELO ¿Cuántos días hay en el mes de septiembre?
Hay treinta días.

1. ¿Cuántos días hay en una semana?

____

2. ¿Cuántas semanas hay en un año?

____

3. ¿Cuántos días hay en el mes de abril?

____

4. ¿Cuántas estaciones hay en el año?

____

5. ¿Cuántos días hay en un año?

____

03-45 Heritage language: *tu español*. The spelling of the words **hay, ay** (an exclamation much like *Oh* in English) and **ahí** (meaning *there*) are often confused because they sound alike. Listen to each sentence and use the context to determine which word is being used.

1. hay ay ahí
2. hay ay ahí
3. hay ay ahí
4. hay ay ahí
5. hay ay ahí

Nota cultural: Las casas "verdes" (Textbook p. 119)

03-46 La España "verde." Select the correct response or responses to each question, based on the information from your textbook.

1. ¿Cuáles de las siguientes regiones de España son parte de la "España verde"?
   ______ Cataluña
   ______ Andalucía
   ______ País Vasco
   ______ Girona
   ______ Asturias
2. ¿En qué parte del país está la "España verde"?
   ______ Norte
   ______ Sur
   ______ Este
   ______ Oeste
3. ¿Por qué se llama esta zona del país "España verde"
   ______ Las personas que viven en esa zona quieren vivir una vida "verde".
   ______ El tiempo y su efecto en el color de los paisajes
   ______ El uso de energías renovables
4. ¿Qué tipos de energías renovables menciona el texto?
   ______ Energía solar
   ______ Energía del viento
   ______ Energía de biomasa
5. ¿Por qué son "verdes" las casas blancas en el sur de España?
   ______ Tienen paneles solares.
   ______ Gracias a su color blanco, hace menos calor en las casas durante el verano.
   ______ Producen entre el 30% y el 50% de su electricidad del viento.
   ______ Es una tradición muy vieja.

Nombre: ______________________ Fecha: ______________________

Escucha (Textbook p. 121)

03-47 Se alquila un dormitorio en una casa. Silvia has a room for rent in her house. This could be a great opportunity for Gabriela. Listen to their conversation, paying special attention to the characteristics that correspond to the house, and then respond to the questions. More than one response may be correct.

1. ¿Dónde está la casa?

   _____ en el centro de la ciudad

   _____ en la universidad

   _____ en una urbanización

   _____ en el centro comercial

2. ¿Qué está cerca de la casa?

   _____ la universidad

   _____ el autobús

   _____ las tiendas

   _____ los restaurantes

3. ¿Qué hay en la casa?

   _____ cinco dormitorios

   _____ dos baños

   _____ tres dormitorios

   _____ seis baños

4. ¿Cuántas salas tiene?

   _____ 1

   _____ 2

   _____ 3

   _____ 12

5. ¿Cuántas personas viven en la casa en este momento?

   _____ 15

   _____ 4

   _____ 5

   _____ 3

6. ¿Cuánto cuesta (*costs*) el alquiler (*rent*)?

   _____ $550,00

   _____ $450,00

   _____ $1.500,00

   _____ $500,00

03-48 Las condiciones del alquiler. Gabriela is very interested in renting a house that she has seen and would like to speak with Silvia, the owner of the house, about the specifics of the rental agreement. Listen to their conversation and then decide if the answers to the following questions are **sí** or **no.**

1. ¿Ofrecen (*do they offer*) un dormitorio para ella solamente? sí no
2. ¿Tiene un baño para ella solamente? sí no
3. ¿Incluye el precio (*does the price include*) del alquiler los gastos (*expenses*) de electricidad? sí no
4. ¿Ofrecen comida? sí no
5. ¿Ofrecen espacio en la cocina para guardar su comida? sí no
6. ¿Tiene que pagar (*pay*) $1.500 de depósito? sí no

¡Conversemos! (Textbook p. 122)

03-49 ¿Y tu casa? Describe your own family's house.

Paso 1.

1. ¿Cuántas habitaciones hay en la casa y cómo son?

____

2. ¿Hay altillo y/o sótano en la casa?

____

3. ¿Cuántos baños hay y cómo son? ¿Hay bañeras y/o duchas en la casa?

____

4. ¿Cuántas salas hay? ¿Hay una sala formal? ¿Hay una informal?

____

5. ¿Cómo es la cocina de la casa?

____

6. ¿Cuáles son tus lugares favoritos de la casa? ¿Por qué son tus lugares favoritos?

____

Paso 2. Now describe your house. Use **hay** to give details about the number of floors, rooms, bedrooms, and bathrooms and use other vocabulary that you have learned in order to describe the style of the house and its rooms, as well as the furniture that is in each room. Finally, make sure to mention in which rooms you spend most of your time, what your favorite places are in the house and what you do in each place. Use at least eight different verbs in your description and use **y, pero,** and **también** to connect your ideas.

Nombre: ______________________________ Fecha: ______________________

Escribe (Textbook p. 123)

03-50 Tu mercadillo. You are about to move abroad for an indefinite period of time. In order to raise money for your move, you have organized a yard sale.

Paso 1. List the kinds of items that you would sell and about how much you would charge for each item.

____

____

____

____

____

____

Paso 2. In order for your yard sale to be a success, you will need to publicize it widely and attractively. Write an ad for your local paper highlighting the most interesting and unique aspects of your yard sale and including important information like when and where it will take place.

____

____

____

____

____

____

Cultura: España (Textbook pp. 124–125)

03-51 Les presento mi país. Select the correct ending for each sentence based on the information in your textbook about Mariela Castañeda Ropero and Spain. More than one option may be correct.

1. El apellido del padre de Mariela es ________.

   ______ Castañeda

   ______ Ropero

2. El apellido de su madre es ________.

   ______ Castañeda

   ______ Ropero

3. Mariela vive en un ________.

   ______ chalet

   ______ casa

   ______ piso

4. A Mariela le gusta la vida en la ciudad porque ________.

   ______ hay muchas cosas para hacer

   ______ hay mucha gente

   ______ hay muchas tiendas

5. Cuando tiene tiempo libre con sus amigos, a Mariela le gusta ________.

   ______ jugar al fútbol

   ______ ir de tapas

   ______ la vida en la capital

   ______ salir a tomar algo

   ______ ver la televisión

6. Mariela y sus amigos hablan ________.

   ______ de política

   ______ de fútbol

   ______ de los equipos españoles

03-52 España. Complete the following statements about Spain, using information from *Capítulo 3*.

1. Las cuatro lenguas que se hablan en España son español, eusquera (vasco), ________________ y ________________.

2. Una organización que ayuda a la gente con discapacidades se llama ________________.

3. Los dos personajes famosos del autor Cervantes son ________________ y ________________.

4. La Alhambra está en la ciudad de ________________, España.

5. Algunos edificios diseñados por Antonio Gaudí están en la ciudad de ________________, España.

Nombre: ______________________ Fecha: ______________________

03-53 Vistas culturales: España. View the video segments in order to complete each part of the activity. You will likely not understand all of the words that you hear, but you should relax because you are capable of understanding more than enough to be able to respond to the questions without difficulty.

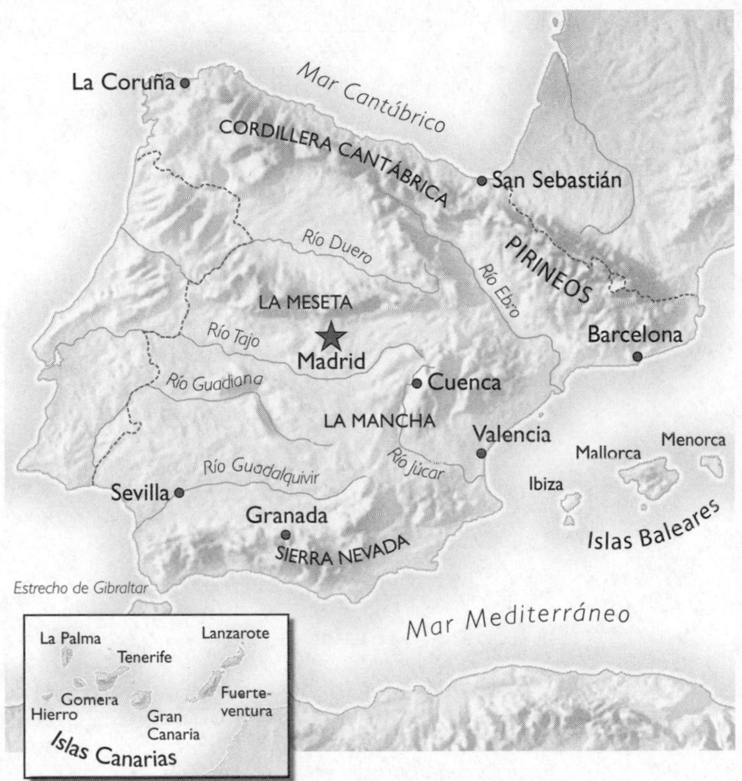

España: Introducción. View the video and then choose the correct response or responses to each question.

1. ¿En qué continente está España?
   ______ África
   ______ América
   ______ Asia
   ______ Europa

2. ¿Cuáles son los países con los que España tiene frontera (*border*)?
   ______ Portugal
   ______ Italia
   ______ Francia
   ______ Andorra

3. ¿Cuántos habitantes tiene España?
   ______ aproximadamente 4.000.000
   ______ aproximadamente 14.000.000
   ______ aproximadamente 40.000.000
   ______ aproximadamente 140.000.000

4. ¿Cuántos kilómetros de costa (*coast*) tiene España?
   ______ casi 1.500
   ______ casi 5.000
   ______ casi 1.5000
   ______ casi 50.000

5. ¿Dónde están las Islas Baleares?
   ______ el Océano Atlántico
   ______ el Mar Cantábrico
   ______ el Mar Mediterráneo

6. ¿En qué continente están las ciudades españolas de Ceuta y Melilla?
   ______ África
   ______ América
   ______ Asia
   ______ Europa

Nombre: ________________________________ Fecha: ________________________

España: La economía de España. View the video and complete each sentence with the correct information.

7. España entra en la Comunidad Económica Europea en el año ________________.

8. El euro ha sido *(has been)* la moneda oficial en España desde el año ________________.

España: Las lenguas de España. View the video and complete each sentence with the correct word.

9. Muchas personas hablan catalán en la región de ________________.

10. En el País Vasco la gente habla español y también ________________.

11. Mucha gente habla gallego en ________________.

España: El clima y el paisaje. View the video and choose the correct response or responses to each question.

12. ¿Qué tiempo hace en el sur (*South*) y en el oeste (*West*) de España?

_____ Hace mucho sol y calor.

_____ Hace mucho calor y llueve mucho.

_____ Hace sol, pero no hace calor.

13. ¿Qué tiempo hace en el interior de España durante el invierno?

_____ Llueve mucho.

_____ Hace mucho frío.

_____ Nieva.

_____ Hace calor.

14. ¿Qué tiempo hace en el interior de España durante el verano?

_____ Llueve mucho.

_____ Hace mucho frío.

_____ Nieva.

_____ Hace calor.

15. ¿De qué color son los paisajes (*landscapes*) en el norte de España?

_____ beige

_____ marrones

_____ verdes

_____ blancos

España: Las fiestas y celebraciones de España. View the video and select the correct response for each question.

16. ¿Dónde celebran la fiesta de San Fermín?
   a. Valencia
   b. Sevilla
   c. Barcelona
   d. Pamplona

17. ¿Dónde celebran las fallas?
   a. Valencia
   b. Sevilla
   c. Barcelona
   d. Pamplona

18. ¿Dónde celebran la fiesta de la Merced?
   a. Valencia
   b. Sevilla
   c. Barcelona
   d. Pamplona

19. ¿Cuándo celebran la fiesta de la Merced?
   a. en verano
   b. en otoño
   c. en invierno
   d. en primavera

Nombre: ______________________________ Fecha: ________________________

Más cultura

03-54 Los jóvenes, el matrimonio y las casas. Read the information about young people, getting engaged and married, and buying homes. Then, answer the questions.

- En muchos lugares del mundo hispano las personas continúan con la tradición de vivir con sus padres hasta celebrar su propio matrimonio. Algunas personas hacen esto porque es parte de la tradición de la familia, otras personas porque es parte de su tradición religiosa, y otras personas lo hacen por razones económicas.
- Muchas personas simplemente no pueden independizarse –vivir independientemente en un apartamento– porque su situación socioeconómica no lo permite. Las casas y los apartamentos cuestan mucho dinero y es importante tener un trabajo y un salario estables si uno quiere alquilar o comprar una vivienda.
- Aunque algunas personas pueden pensar lo contrario, hay muchas ventajas (*advantages*) para la persona que vive con su familia. No tiene que hacer muchos quehaceres de la casa porque hay más personas en casa para ayudar. También es bueno pasar mucho tiempo con personas importantes; puede verlas y hablar con ella todos los días.
- En el mundo hispano también hay cada vez más (*more and more*) gente joven que quiere independizarse rápidamente. Algunas personas alquilan o compran un apartamento después de terminar sus estudios en la universidad.
- Muchos bancos ofrecen cuentas de ahorro (*savings accounts*) especiales para los jóvenes interesados en ahorrar (*save up*) para comprar casa. Algunos bancos también ofrecen hipotecas (*mortgages*) especiales, con condiciones muy favorables, que son exclusivamente para jóvenes.

1. ¿Cómo secomparan las tradiciones de tu familia con las tradiciones hispanas? ¿Tienes planes de vivir con tus padres después de terminar tus estudios?

____

____

____

____

____

2. ¿Tienes amigos de otras culturas que tienen tradiciones similares a las tradiciones hispanas? ¿De dónde son?

____

____

____

____

____

3. ¿Tienes una cuenta de ahorro especial para jóvenes? ¿Tiene tu banco hipotecas especiales para jóvenes?

4. ¿Crees que es difícil para los jóvenes independizarse en los Estados Unidos? ¿En tu ciudad o estado? ¿Por qué o por qué no?

03-55 Heritage Language: *tu mundo hispano*. Reflect on and write about the following issues in relation to a specific Hispanic culture. If you are of Spanish-speaking heritage, discuss these issues with members of your own family. If you are not, interview Spanish-speaking friends, relatives, or fellow students on your campus in order to find out more about their practices and perspectives. Write answers for each of the questions.

1. ¿En tu país, cuándo se independizan los jóvenes normalmente? ¿Por qué? Con la situación ecónomica y de trabajo actuales *(present)*, ¿es fácil o difícil independizarse?

2. ¿En tu país, ofrecen los bancos cuentas especiales y/o hipotecas especiales para los jóvenes? Si es así, ¿cómo son? Si no, ¿por qué crees que no los ofrecen?

03-56 Los hombres, las mujeres y los quehaceres. Read the following information about women and men and their household chores, and then answer the questions.

- Como en muchos lugares del mundo anglosajón (*English-speaking*), en muchos lugares del mundo hispano, la distribución del trabajo en casa no es muy justa (*fair*) y en muchas casos las mujeres hacen más trabajo que los hombres.
- Afortunadamente, poco a poco esta situación cambia (*changes*). Hoy en día hay más mujeres que trabajan fuera de (*outside of*) la casa, y simplemente no pueden hacer todo el trabajo dentro de (*inside of*) la casa también. Muchos hombres comprenden la situación y ahora (*now*) hacen más quehaceres domésticos que antes.
- Otra solución muy común es buscar ayuda (*to look for help*) profesional. Muchas familias usan parte de su dinero para pagar a "una asistenta" —una persona que viene a casa regularmente para hacer o ayudar con los quehaceres domésticos.

1. ¿En tu familia, qué quehaceres hacen las mujeres y qué hacen los hombres? ¿Hay una distribución justa o injusta? ¿Por qué?

____

____

____

____

____

2. ¿En general en tu familia, trabajan todas las mujeres y todos los hombres fuera de la casa?

____

____

3. ¿En tu familia, hay una asistenta para ayudar con los quehaceres de casa? ¿Por qué sí o por qué no? Si es así, ¿cuáles son sus responsabilidades?

____

____

____

____

____

4. ¿Quieres tener una asistenta en el futuro? ¿Por qué sí o por qué no?

____

____

____

____

____

5. ¿Crees que la situación de tu familia es similar a la situación de muchas familias en los Estados Unidos? ¿Por qué sí o por qué no?

____

____

____

____

____

Nombre: ______________________ Fecha: ______________________

Ambiciones siniestras

Episodio 3

Lectura: *El concurso* (Textbook p. 126)

03-57 Alejandra, Pili y el concurso. Read the episode "El concurso" and then answer the questions. Use brief but complete sentences making sure not to repeat the known subject, as in the model.

MODELO ¿Por qué quiere Alejandra mirar su e-mail?
Quiere ver si tiene un mensaje de Pili.

1. ¿Cómo está Pili?

   ____

2. ¿Cuántos años tiene Pili?

   ____

3. ¿Quién es Peter?

   ____

4. ¿Cuántos años tiene Peter?

   ____

5. ¿Cómo son los padres de Alejandra y Pili?

   ____

6. ¿Van a estar contentos los padres de Pili esta noche?

   ____

Nombre: ______________________________ Fecha: ______________________

Video: *¡Tienes una gran oportunidad!* (Textbook p. 128)

03-58 Hipótesis sobre las casas y los dormitorios de los muchachos. In this episode Marisol sees Lupe's apartment and they speak about her bedroom, and Cisco and Eduardo see photographs of each other's homes. You already know some information about the four characters. Answer the questions based on what you know.

¿Cómo crees que son los dormitorios de Marisol y Lupe? ¿Qué tipo de cosas crees que tienen? Escribe tus ideas.

1. El dormitorio de Marisol

____

____

2. El dormitorio de Lupe

____

____

¿Cómo crees que son las casas de las familias de Eduardo y Cisco? ¿Por qué o porqué no? Escribe tus ideas.

1. La casa de la familia de Eduardo

____

____

2. La casa de la familia de Cisco

____

____

Nombre: ______________________ Fecha: ______________________

03-59 Las casas y los dormitorios de los muchachos.

Paso 1. Read the statements, view the episode and then indicate to whom each statement refers.

1. Mi dormitorio tiene dos armarios. Lupe Marisol Eduardo Cisco
2. Mi dormitorio tiene una cama grande. Lupe Marisol Eduardo Cisco
3. Tengo carteles con monumentos de España en mi dormitorio. Lupe Marisol Eduardo Cisco
4. En mi dormitorio hay un sillón. Lupe Marisol Eduardo Cisco

Paso 2. Read the statements, view the episode again and then indicate to whom each statement refers.

5. Mi casa tiene una piscina (*pool*) impresionante. Lupe Marisol Eduardo Cisco
6. Mi dormitorio es muy pequeño. Lupe Marisol Eduardo Cisco
7. Mi casa es muy grande y el jardín tiene muchas flores de diferentes colores. Lupe Marisol Eduardo Cisco
8. Mi dormitorio tiene una mesa para la computadora. Lupe Marisol Eduardo Cisco

03-60 ¿Comprendes?

Indicate to whom these statements about the details of the video refer. If necessary, view the video again.

1. No sé dónde están mis apuntes para una de mis clases. Lupe Marisol Eduardo Cisco
2. Estoy cansado. Lupe Marisol Eduardo Cisco
3. Me gustan mucho Barcelona, Madrid y Sevilla. Lupe Marisol Eduardo Cisco
4. Son muchos ejercicios pero no son muy difíciles. Lupe Marisol Eduardo Cisco
5. Tengo un dormitorio en la casa de mis padres. Lupe Marisol Eduardo Cisco
6. Tengo clase en menos de una hora. Lupe Marisol Eduardo Cisco
7. Conozco Estados Unidos, Canadá y México. Lupe Marisol Eduardo Cisco
8. La casa de mi familia es muy grande. Lupe Marisol Eduardo Cisco

03-61 Después del video. Consider the following questions and then write a paragraph in English about how the different characters react to the mysterious message.

Which of the characters seemed most surprised to receive the mysterious message, and which seemed least surprised? Which characters seem to think the message might be legitimate, and which are more skeptical? With which perspective do you identify most? Why? Which of the characters do you think will respond to the message? Explain the reasons for your hypotheses.

____

____

____

____

____

____

____

____

____

Comunidades

03-62 Experiential Learning: Las viviendas en España. Research the current situation of the housing market in Spain. Visit a Spanish real estate website (such as idealista.com or www.donpiso.es) and search for a house or apartment in at least five different cities. Make sure to include Madrid and Barcelona, as well as at least one city on the coast, one in **Andalucía,** one in the **País Vasco.** Bring the listings to class so that you will also have the chance to present your findings to your classmates.

03-63 Service Learning: Casas para todos. Contact Habitat for Humanity or another organization focused on helping to create housing options for people in need. Volunteer to create outreach or promotional materials in Spanish about the organization's most recent projects. Brainstorm about how to promote their work effectively in Spanish and bring a draft of your preliminary ideas to class so that you and your classmates can share your ideas and create final drafts in groups.

Nombre: ______________________ Fecha: ______________________

04-03 ¿Cuáles son tus lugares favoritos?

Paso 1. Answer the following questions using complete sentences.

MODELO ¿Cuál es tu supermercado favorito?
Mi supermercado favorito es Kings.

1. ¿Cuál es tu restaurante favorito?

   ____.

2. ¿Cuál es tu café favorito?

   ____.

3. ¿Cuál es tu bar o tu club favorito?

   ____.

4. ¿Cuál es tu almacén favorito?

   ____.

5. ¿Cuál es tu cine favorito?

   ____.

6. ¿Cuál es tu museo favorito?

   ____.

Paso 2. Choose four places from the following list. Write notes about what you enjoy doing at each location and when you generally spend time there.

el cine
el centro estudiantil
el gimnasio
el centro comercial
el café
el museo
el restaurante
la residencia estudiantil
tu cuarto

7. ____

   ____

   ____

   ____

Paso 3. Describe the four places you mentioned in **Paso 2**, the activities that you enjoy doing there, when you generally spend time there, and with whom you generally spend time at these places. Be careful to use the correct forms of the verbs.

04-04 Heritage Language: *tu español*. The terms you have learned so far to describe different places around town are common and easily understood throughout the Spanish-speaking world. Other terms are also used to describe these places. Many of these names are formed the same way as **librería** and **cafetería**: by combining the name of the main product that they sell with the suffix **–ería**.

Paso 1. Use this knowledge about place names as you listen to each place of business in order to match each place with its correct description. You may also use the Appendix 3 **También se dice** section of your textbook to help you.

1. ________	a. tienda de muebles
2. ________	b. tienda en la que venden frutas como bananas, kiwis, etc.
3. ________	c. tienda en la que venden papel, bolígrafos, etc.
4. ________	d. tienda de pan (*bread*)
5. ________	e. restaurante que se especializa en pizza
6. ________	f. tienda en la que venden perfume
7. ________	g. tienda en la que venden pescado (*fish*)
8. ________	h. tienda en la que venden flores (como rosas)
9. ________	i. tienda en la que venden pasteles (*cakes*, *pies*, *pastries*)
10. ________	j. tienda en la que venden helado (*ice cream*)

Paso 2. While many people still do most of their shopping in small stores like those mentioned in **Paso 1**, with the arrival of larger stores and shopping centers, others have changed this custom. Ask a relative, friend, or fellow student of Spanish-speaking heritage about the practices of their own families in Spanish-speaking countries. Write **Sí**, **No**, or **Depende** (*it depends*) to answer the following questions about their habits.

11. Do they usually buy bread every morning at a **panadería**?

____

12. Do they buy their fruit and vegetables at a **frutería**?

____

13. Do they buy fish at a **pescadería**?

____

14. Do they shop at **pastelerías**?

____

15. Do they like to shop at small, specialized stores or do they prefer to go to large stores that carry a wide variety of items?

____

Nombre: ______________________________ Fecha: ______________________

Pronunciación: The letters *c* and *z* (Textbook p. 135)

1. Before the vowels **a, o,** and **u,** and when followed by a consonant, the Spanish **c** is pronounced like the *c* in the English word *car.*

2. Before the vowels **e** and **i,** the Spanish **c** is pronounced like the *s* in the English word *seal.*

3. The Spanish **z** is pronounced like the *s* in the English word *seal.*

04-05 Tu pronunciación.

Paso 1. Palabras. Listen to the Spanish-speaker's pronunciation of the following words, and practice your own pronunciation of them.

1. ciudad
2. lápiz
3. almacén
4. cibercafé

Paso 2. Oraciones. Listen to the affirmations and questions, and then practice your pronunciation of them. Pay special attention to your pronunciation of the letters **c** and **z,** and also to your pronunciation of the vowels (**a, e, i, o, u**).

5. Sé que quieres ir al cine con Cecilia, Celia y Catarina.
6. ¿Sabes a qué hora cierra el almacén?
7. ¿Conoces los museos de Cáceres?
8. Necesito saber en qué zona de la ciudad está tu casa.

Paso 3. Trabalenguas. Listen to the tongue-twisters, and then practice your own pronunciation of them. Pay special attention to your pronunciation of the letters **c** and **z,** and also of the vowels (**a, e, i, o, u**).

9. ¿Cómo como? ¡Como, como, como!
10. Cuando cuentas cuentos nunca cuentas cuántos cuentos cuentas.
11. Historia es la narración sucesiva de los sucesos que suceden sucesivamente en la sucesión sucesiva del tiempo.
12. Paco Pizarro Pérez pinta pinturas preciosas para personas poderosas en sus palacios. Para pobres pinta poco porque pagan poco precio.

Nombre: ______________________ Fecha: ______________________

04-06 Refranes populares.

Paso 1. Read the following information about two popular sayings in Spanish, and then answer the questions.

"La caridad bien entendida empieza por casa".

1. La palabra "caridad" significa *charity* en inglés y "empieza" es del verbo "empezar" que significa *to begin*. Gracias al Capítulo 3, comprendes la palabra "casa". Este refrán también existe en inglés. ¿Conoces el refrán en inglés que tiene esas palabras o palabras muy similares? Escribe el refrán en inglés.

____

2. ¿Puedes describir el mensaje de este refrán? Describe en inglés qué mensaje interpretas en este refrán.

____

____

____

"En boca cerrada no entran moscas".

3. La palabra "boca" significa *mouth* y una mosca es un tipo de insecto. La palabra "cerrada" viene del verbo **cerrar** ("cierren los libros", "abran los libros"). Aquí la palabra tiene un rol descriptivo, "cerrada" describe cómo está la boca (como una puerta o una ventana, una boca puede estar cerrada o abierta). ¿Puedes describir el mensaje de este refrán? Describe en inglés qué mensaje podemos interpretar en este refrán.

____

____

____

4. Este refrán no tiene una versión en inglés, pero tú puedes inventar una versión. Escribe tu versión en inglés del refrán.

____

Paso 2. Listen to the sayings, and then practice your own pronunciation of them. Pay special attention to your pronunciation of the letters **c** and **z**, and also of the vowels (**a, e, i, o, u**).

5. "La caridad bien entendida empieza por casa".

6. "En boca cerrada no entran moscas".

Nombre: ______________________ Fecha: ______________________

Nota cultural: Actividades cotidianas: Las compras y el paseo
(Textbook p. 136)

04-07 Las ciudades y los pueblos. Based upon what you read in your textbook about daily activities in cities and small towns, select the correct response(s) to complete the following sentences.

1. Según el texto, muchos estadounidenses y muchas de las personas de las ciudades grandes de los países hispanohablantes hacen muchas de sus compras en ________________.
   el centro de la ciudad
   tiendas especializadas
   centros comerciales

2. Según el texto, muchas de las personas que viven en pueblos pequeños hacen muchas de sus compras en ________________.
   el centro de la ciudad
   tiendas especializadas
   centros comerciales

3. Algunos lugares importantes que hay en el centro de la ciudad son ________________.
   Maxi Bodega
   el mercado
   muchas tiendas

4. En el centro de la ciudad hay personas de diferentes ________________.
   países
   culturas
   clases sociales

5. Las actividades que hace la gente en la plaza son ________________.
   correr
   conversar
   pasear

6. Las personas que viven en los pueblos pequeños frecuentemente pasean por ________________.
   los parques
   las plazas
   el campo

7. En los pueblos normalmente hay más actividad ________________.
   de lunes a viernes
   los sábados y los domingos
   los lunes

Nombre: ______________________ Fecha: ______________________

04-08 ¿Y tu pueblo o ciudad? Describe your city or town and common daily activities there.

Paso 1. Answer the following questions; it is not necessary to use complete sentences.

1. ¿Eres de un pueblo o de una ciudad? ¿Es grande o pequeño/a?

   ____

2. ¿Cómo es similar a una ciudad grande de los países hispanohablantes? ¿Cómo es similar a un pueblo pequeño de un país hispanohablante? ¿Cómo es diferente?

   ____

3. ¿Qué lugares importantes o interesantes hay en tu pueblo / ciudad?

   ____

4. ¿Qué hace la gente en los lugares importantes?

   ____

5. ¿Dónde hacen muchas personas la compra?

   ____

6. ¿Dónde pasea la gente de tu pueblo / tu ciudad?

   ____

7. ¿Cuándo hay mucha actividad por las calles de tu pueblo / ciudad?

   ____

8. ¿Qué te gusta de tu pueblo / ciudad? ¿Qué no te gusta?

   ____

Paso 2. Now give an oral description of your town or city, its places of interest, and the common things that people do there. Mention some things about your city or town that you like and other things that you do not care for.

Nombre: ______________________ Fecha: ______________________

Gramática

2. *Saber* y *conocer*: Stating whom and what is known (Textbook p. 137)

04-09 ¡Cuánto sabes! Listen to the questions and then write your affirmative responses, using the cities in the word bank. Be sure to follow the sentence structure of the model closely.

MODELO ¿Sabes cuál es la capital de Ecuador?
Sí, lo sé. Quito es la capital de Ecuador.

Madrid	~~Quito~~	Ciudad de México	Tegucigalpa
Buenos Aires	Ciudad de Guatemala	San Salvador	

1. ______________________
2. ______________________
3. ______________________
4. ______________________
5. ______________________
6. ______________________

04-10 El mundo de la música. Rosario and her friends are very talented and would like to start a rock band. Complete the description about them using the correct forms of ***saber*** or ***conocer***.

Todos mis amigos y yo tenemos muchos talentos; nosotros (1) ____________ hacer muchas cosas. Por ejemplo, yo (2) ____________ tocar el piano, mi amigo Pablo (3) ____________ tocar la guitarra, Sara (4) ____________ tocar la batería (*drums*), y nuestros amigos Mario y Teresa (5) ____________ cantar (*to sing*) muy bien. Nosotros queremos tener un grupo de música rock. ¿Quieres ser parte de nuestro grupo? ¿(6) ____________ tú tocar el bajo (*bass guitar*)?

Nosotros tenemos gustos (*tastes*) musicales muy diversos y eso puede ser muy interesante para nuestro grupo. Yo (7) ____________ mucha música latina. Pablo y Teresa (8) ____________ mucha música jazz y Mario (9) ____________ mucha música rock de los años setenta. Susana trabaja para una compañía discográfica y por eso, (10) ____________ a muchos agentes que nos pueden ayudar.

04-11 ¿Qué saben y qué conocen? Pablo is a tourist in Antigua, Guatemala, but does not have a map and has lost his tour book of the city. Complete his conversation with Laura using the correct forms of ***saber*** or ***conocer***.

PABLO: Hola, buenas tardes. Estoy un poco perdido (*lost*), ¿puedes ayudarme?

LAURA: Claro, yo soy de Antigua y (1) ____________________ muy bien la ciudad.

PABLO: ¡Qué bien! Muchas gracias. ¿(2) ____________________ dónde está el Museo de Arte Colonial?

LAURA: Sí, (3) ____________________ exactamente dónde está —al final de esta calle, cerca de la Plaza Mayor.

PABLO: ¿(4)____________________ cuánto cuesta (*costs*) entrar en el museo?

LAURA: Sí, creo que cuesta 10,00 quetzales para las personas que no son de Guatemala.

PABLO: También necesito comprar otro libro sobre la ciudad; ¿(5) ____________________ una buena librería por aquí cerca (*close by*)?

LAURA: Sí, también hay una librería por esa calle; tienen buenos libros a buenos precios. Si te gustan los libros, también tenemos otro museo interesante aquí.

PABLO: Sí, ya lo (6) ____________________ —el Museo del Libro Antiguo. Quiero visitarlo hoy también. ¿Está cerca del Museo de Arte, ¿no?

LAURA: Sí, y en el Museo de Arte te pueden dar un mapa para orientarte mejor. Si después de ir a los museos tienes hambre, (7) ____________________ un restaurante que está en esa zona también; es uno de los mejores restaurantes de la ciudad. Si quieres, ahora voy contigo al museo y te enseño dónde está.

PABLO: ¡Qué bien!

04-12 Heritage Language: *tu español*. Because the letters **s, z,** and the soft **c** are pronounced exactly the same way in all Spanish-speaking countries except for Spain, it can be difficult to remember how to spell different forms of the verb ***conocer***. Listen to each sentence, and then write the correct spelling of the conjugation of the verb used in the sentence.

1. ____________________

2. ____________________

3. ____________________

4. ____________________

5. ____________________

Nombre: ______________________ Fecha: ______________________

Vocabulario

3. ¿Qué tienen que hacer? ¿Qué pasa? Relating common obligations and activities (Textbook p. 140)

04-13 Asociaciones. Associate the following phrases with the most logical expressions.

1. ¡No sé dónde está mi mamá! ______
2. Soy muy filosófico. ______
3. Por fin descubro (*discover*) dónde está mi mamá. ______
4. Tengo una dieta muy sana y saludable (*healthy*). ______
5. Soy principiante (*beginner*). ______
6. Soy una persona que persiste mucho. ______
7. Vivo una vida loca (*wild life*). ______

a. Pienso mucho en temas muy profundos (*profound*).
b. Almuerzo bien todos los días.
c. Pierdo a una persona importante.
d. Voy a la discoteca todas las noches y después duermo hasta muy tarde (*until very late*) todos los días.
e. Comienzo una cosa nueva.
f. Encuentro a una persona importante.
g. Sigo y sigo y sigo y sigo.

04-14 Al que algo quiere, algo le cuesta. Associate the following affirmations about what people would like to do with the statements that describe what they have to do in order to reach their goals.

1. No quiero tener hambre por las tardes. ______
2. Quiero tomar buenos apuntes durante las clases. ______
3. Quiero ser más independiente. ______
4. Quiero entender un concepto muy especializado y muy complicado. ______
5. Quiero empezar a estudiar ahora. ______
6. Estoy muy cansado de estudiar y quiero descansar (*rest*) un poco. ______
7. Quiero poder concentrarme mejor y tener más energía. ______

a. Tengo que pedir la ayuda de un especialista en la materia.
b. Tengo que cerrar mi libro y mis apuntes y dormir la siesta.
c. Tengo que almorzar bien todos los días.
d. Tengo que encontrar mi libro.
e. Tengo que entender qué dicen los profesores.
f. Tengo que dormir un mínimo de ocho horas todas las noches y hacer ejercicio un mínimo de tres días todas las semanas.
g. Tengo que pensar por mí mismo (*my own self*) y tomar mis propias (*my own*) decisiones.

04-15 ¿Qué tenemos que hacer? Complete the sentences with the correct form of ***tener que*** and with the most logical verb from the word bank. Follow the model.

pedir	almorzar	encontrar
pensar	volver	~~dormir~~

MODELO Cuando tenemos sueño, *tenemos que dormir*.

1. Cuando tienes hambre, ______________.
2. Cuando salgo de casa y no tengo mi mochila, ______________ a mi casa para tener la mochila para mis clases.
3. Cuando necesitamos tomar una decisión importante, ______________ mucho antes de tomar la decisión.
4. Cuando no sé dónde está mi libro, ______________ el libro si quiero estudiar.
5. Cuando ellos no saben la respuesta correcta, ______________ ayuda a su profesor o a uno de sus compañeros.

04-16 Heritage Language: *tu español*. As you know, because the letters **s, z,** and the soft **c** are pronounced exactly the same way in all Spanish-speaking countries except for Spain, it can be difficult to remember how to spell some words. Heighten your own awareness of how the verbs you have just learned are spelled. Listen to each sentence containing these new verbs, and then select the letter that each contains.

1. s soft c z
2. s soft c z
3. s soft c z
4. s soft c z
5. s soft c z

Gramática

4. Los verbos con cambio de raíz: Expressing actions (Textbook p. 142)

04-17 Categorías correctas. Choose what type of stem-changing verb each of the following is. If it is not stem-changing, then select **no tiene cambio de raíz**.

1. cerrar
   a. e → ie
   b. e → i
   c. o → ue
   d. no tiene cambio de raíz

2. mostrar
   a. e → ie
   b. e → i
   c. o → ue
   d. no tiene cambio de raíz

3. contestar
   a. e → ie
   b. e → i
   c. o → ue
   d. no tiene cambio de raíz

4. repetir
   a. e → ie
   b. e → i
   c. o → ue
   d. no tiene cambio de raíz

5. arreglar
   a. e → ie
   b. e → i
   c. o → ue
   d. no tiene cambio de raíz

6. poder
   a. e → ie
   b. e → i
   c. o → ue
   d. no tiene cambio de raíz

7. pedir
   a. e → ie
   b. e → i
   c. o → ue
   d. no tiene cambio de raíz

8. mentir
   a. e → ie
   b. e → i
   c. o → ue
   d. no tiene cambio de raíz

9. dormir
   a. e → ie
   b. e → i
   c. o → ue
   d. no tiene cambio de raíz

10. tomar
    a. e → ie
    b. e → i
    c. o → ue
    d. no tiene cambio de raíz

Nombre: ______________________ Fecha: ______________________

04-18 Un proyecto importante.

Susana and José have to do an important project for class together.

Paso 1. Listen to their conversation and then indicate if the following affirmations are **Cierto** or **Falso**.

1. Susana no quiere trabajar en el proyecto a las 3:00 porque tiene que trabajar. Cierto Falso
2. Susana trabaja en un restaurante. Cierto Falso
3. Susana tiene que empezar a trabajar a las 7:00. Cierto Falso
4. Después de trabajar Susana quiere salir con sus amigas. Cierto Falso
5. José prefiere trabajar en el proyecto a las 5:00. Cierto Falso

Paso 2. Listen to the conversation once more. Then, rewrite the selected portions of the false statements in order to make them true. For those that are already true, leave the statement as it is.

6. Susana no quiere trabajar en el proyecto <u>a las 3:00</u> porque tiene que trabajar.
7. Susana trabaja en <u>un restaurante</u>.
8. Susana tiene que empezar a trabajar <u>a las 7:00</u>.
9. Después de trabajar Susana quiere <u>salir con sus amigas</u>.
10. José prefiere trabajar en el proyecto <u>a las 5:00</u>.

04-19 ¿Qué quieren hacer?

Listen to the conversation between Ana and Carlos about what they and their friends would like to do. Then, indicate which of the two couples would like to do each activity.

1. ir al cine Ana y Carlos Emilia y Saúl
2. caminar por el parque Ana y Carlos Emilia y Saúl
3. ver una película en casa Ana y Carlos Emilia y Saúl
4. bailar Ana y Carlos Emilia y Saúl
5. tomar algo en un bar Ana y Carlos Emilia y Saúl
6. ir a un restaurante Ana y Carlos Emilia y Saúl

Nombre: ______________________________ Fecha: ______________________

04-20 Crucigrama. Complete the crossword puzzle with the correct forms of the verbs, based upon the pronouns provided.

1. ustedes / empezar
2. ellos / perder
3. tú / devolver
4. tú / demostrar
5. nosotros / recordar
6. ellos / preferir
7. nosotros / recomendar
8. yo / encontrar
9. yo / cerrar
10. ellos / almorzar

11. nosotros / repetir

12. nosotros / seguir

04-21 ¿Cuál es la forma correcta? Your friend from Spanish class needs some help because he does not recall all of the forms of some verbs. Write the correct responses to his questions.

MODELO You hear: ¿Cuál es la forma correcta del verbo tener para el pronombre "ellos"?
You write: *tienen*

1. ____________
2. ____________
3. ____________
4. ____________
5. ____________
6. ____________
7. ____________
8. ____________
9. ____________
10. ____________

04-22 Preferencias y opiniones diferentes. Rosario and Paulo are dating, but often have very different preferences and opinions. Complete the paragraph about them by writing the correct form of the correct verb. Be careful, not all of the verbs need to be conjugated.

preferir	entender	recomendar
querer	empezar	pensar

Rosario siempre (1) ____________ (entender / querer) ir al cine, pero Paulo (2) ____________ (preferir / empezar) el teatro. Paulo (3) ____________ (empezar / pensar) que siempre hacen lo que a Rosario le gusta y al principio (*beginning*) de la conversación Rosario no comprende sus frustraciones. Paulo le explica (*explains*) a Rosario su situación y después Rosario (4) ____________ (preferir / entender) por qué él no está contento. Rosario (5) ____________ (pensar / recomendar) tener una conversación calmada y tranquila para hablar de los problemas y resolver el conflicto. Después de hablar, todo está mejor. Rosario y Paulo deciden que tienen que (6) ____________ (empezar / pensar) a hacer más actividades que les gusten a los dos y no solamente (*only*) a ella.

Nombre: ______________________ Fecha: ______________________

04-26 ¿Adónde van? Complete the sentences using the correct forms of the verb ***ir*** and the most logical places from the word bank, following the model.

~~al cine~~	al banco	al supermercado	a un restaurante elegante
al centro comercial	a correos	al museo	a la biblioteca

MODELO Tengo que ver la nueva película de Guillermo del Toro;
voy al cine.

1. Marta y Sara tienen que encontrar libros sobre (*about*) la literatura cubana; ______________.
2. Tenemos que comprar comida para la casa; ______________.
3. Julio y su novia quieren tener una noche romántica; ______________.
4. Quiero comprar el nuevo disco compacto de Julieta Venegas; ______________.
5. Quieres ver unas pinturas de unos artistas interesantes; ______________.
6. Necesito dinero para comprar materiales para mis clases; ______________.
7. Teresa y yo tenemos que mandar unas cartas; ______________.

04-27 Heritage Language: *tu español.*

Paso 1. Adriana would like to know about your favorite places. Listen to her questions and then give your responses.

MODELO You hear: ¿Adónde vas cuando tienes ganas de bailar?
You say: *Cuando tengo ganas de bailar voy a una discoteca.*

1. …
2. …
3. …
4. …
5. …
6. …
7. …

Paso 2. Now interview a relative, friend, or fellow student who is of Spanish-speaking heritage and find out about that person's favorite places. Ask the person the same questions that Adriana asked you and write the person's responses.

8. ____
9. ____
10. ____
11. ____
12. ____
13. ____
14. ____

Paso 3. Comparatively describe your favorite pastimes and places with those of the person that you interviewed. What do you have in common? What kind of differences characterize your preferences? Are the differences more a result of cultural difference or of age, generational, or other difference?

Gramática

6. *Ir* + *a* + infinitivo: Conveying what will happen in the future
(Textbook p. 147)

04-28 Los horóscopos. Read the horoscopes, and then complete the answers to the questions using the correct forms of the expression ***ir* + *a* + infinitivo.**

Virgo

Este mes va a ser muy bueno para ti. Vas a tener suerte (*luck*) en el amor y en el trabajo. Tus amigos van a demostrar que son buenos y que eres muy importante para ellos.

Acuario

Este mes no va a ser el mejor mes del año para ti. Vas a tener problemas en el amor, y dificultades en el trabajo. No vas a tener mucho dinero, va a ser muy importante ser prudente.

Libra

Tu situación amorosa va a estar muy bien este mes. Si no tienes novio/a, este mes vas a encontrar tu pareja perfecta; si tienes pareja, este mes va a ser maravilloso y muy romántico. Este mes vas a comprar algo que cuesta mucho dinero y que va a cambiar tu vida.

Piscis

Tu situación sentimental va a ser muy estable este mes. Tu situación económica va a mejorar (*improve*) mucho y vas a poder comprar algunas cosas muy importantes. Vas a tener nuevas y muy buenas oportunidades en el trabajo. También vas a conocer nuevos países.

MODELO ¿Quiénes van a comprar cosas importantes?
Las personas de Libra y de Piscis van a comprar cosas importantes.

1. ¿Quiénes no van a tener un mes muy bueno?

   ______________________ un mes muy bueno.

2. ¿Quiénes van a tener suerte con el dinero?

   ______________________ suerte con el dinero.

3. ¿Quiénes van a tener una situación económica difícil este mes?

   ______________________ una situación económica difícil este mes.

4. ¿Quiénes van a tener éxito en su trabajo?

   ______________________ éxito en su trabajo.

5. ¿Quiénes van a tener buenas experiencias con sus amigos?

   ______________________ buenas experiencias con sus amigos.

6. ¿Quiénes van a tener dificultades en su vida amorosa?

   ______________________ dificultades en su vida amorosa.

7. ¿Quiénes van a ir a otros países?

   ______________________ a otros países.

Nombre: ______________________ Fecha: ______________________

04-29 ¿Qué van a hacer? Create logical sentences using one component from each column and the correct forms of the expression ***ir + a* + infinitivo**, following the model. You may use each expression from the table only once. NOTE: The numbers in the first column correspond to the question numbers below.

MODELO Yo *voy a ir a la universidad*, y allí *voy a estudiar para las clases.*

1. ir al gimnasio	hacer	unas pinturas interesantes
2. ir al centro comercial	almorzar	ayuda
3. ir al museo	pedir	pizza
4. ir a la biblioteca	ver	libros
5. ir a correos	devolver	un regalo (*gift*)
6. ir a un restaurante	comprar	unas cartas
7. ir a la oficina de nuestro profesor	mandar	pilates

1. Paula ______________________, y allí ______________________.
2. Clara y yo ______________________, y allí ______________________ para mi prima que cumple años.
3. María ______________________, y allí ______________________.
4. Pedro y tú ______________________, y allí ______________________.
5. Tú ______________________, y allí ______________________.
6. Santi y Marta ______________________, y allí ______________________.
7. Claudio y yo ______________________, y allí ______________________.

Nombre: ______________________ Fecha: ______________________

04-30 Heritage Language: *tu español.*

Paso 1. Take notes about where you and your friends are going to go and what you are going to do next weekend. Do not write complete sentences.

Paso 2. Now use your notes from **Paso 1**, the **Vocabulario útil** below, and expressions with ***ir* + *a* + infinitivo** to describe where you and your friends are going to go and what you are going to do next weekend.

primero *first*	después *afterwards*	entonces *then*
a continuación *right after that*	luego *later on*	finalmente *finally*

Paso 3. Now interview at least two relatives, friends, or fellow students of Spanish-speaking heritage about where they and their friends are going to go and what they are going to do next weekend. Do not write complete sentences.

Paso 4. Now comparatively describe your plans and those of the two people that you interviewed. Be careful to use the correct forms of ***ir* + *a* + infinitivo** in your description.

Nombre: ______________________________ Fecha: ______________________

Vocabulario

7. Servicios a la comunidad: Imparting information about service opportunities (Textbook p. 149)

04-31 Asociaciones. For each item related to volunteerism, mark the places with which it is associated. In some cases there is more than one correct answer.

1. la tienda de campaña
   el campamento de niños
   la campaña política
   la residencia de ancianos

2. dar un paseo
   el campamento de niños
   la campaña política
   la residencia de ancianos

3. la persona mayor
   el campamento de niños
   la campaña política
   la residencia de ancianos

4. ir de excursión
   el campamento de niños
   la campaña política
   la residencia de ancianos

5. apoyar a un candidato
   el campamento de niños
   la campaña política
   la residencia de ancianos

6. hacer objetos de artesanía
   el campamento de niños
   la campaña política
   la residencia de ancianos

7. circular una petición
   el campamento de niños
   la campaña política
   la residencia de ancianos

Nombre: ______________________ Fecha: ______________________

04-32 Crucigrama. Complete the crossword puzzle with the correct words, based upon the definitions provided.

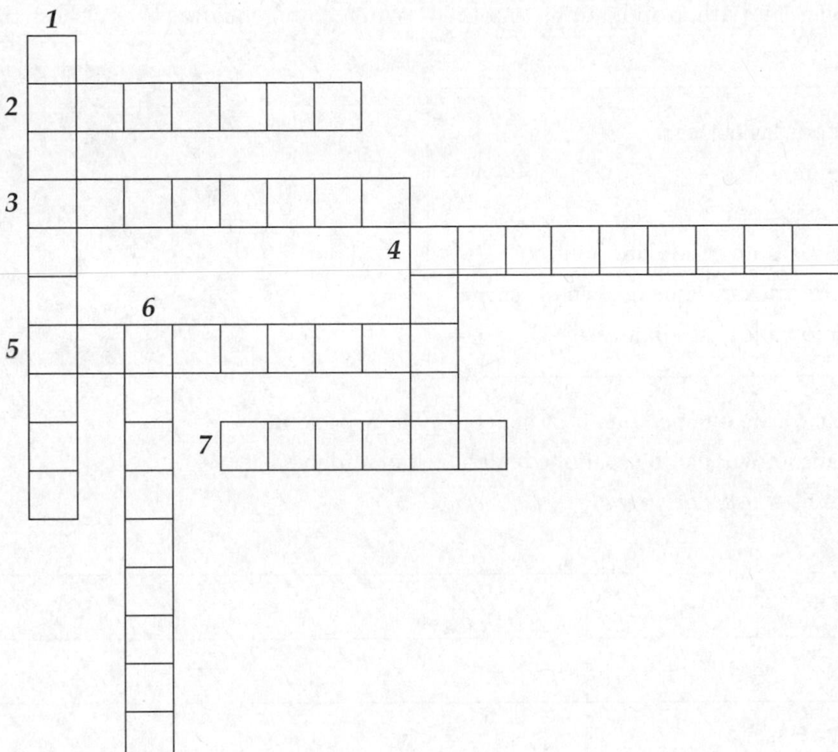

Vertical

1. lugar para los niños en donde hacen muchas actividades variadas y divertidas

4. pequeño vehículo que la gente usa para viajar por el agua

6. un hombre que ayuda a otras personas a tomar decisiones, a resolver problemas en diferentes situaciones

Horizontal

2. un hombre mayor

3. documento que circulamos y firmamos (*we sign*) cuando queremos expresar nuestras opiniones y preferencias políticas

4. una mujer que se presenta a las elecciones porque quiere ser presidenta, senadora o congresista

5. ir a un lugar interesante o diferente para conocerlo o para pasar el día; ir de ______________________

7. sinónimo de **ayudar** o **endorsar**

04-33 ¿Qué debemos hacer en nuestra comunidad? Agustín and his friends want to help out in their community, but need help in deciding how to do so. Listen to what they say about their personalities, lifestyles, and other obligations, and then write recommendations about how they can serve their community.

repartir comidas por las tardes
dar clases de artesanía
trabajar como consejero/a
organizar papeles para un candidato político
ir a la residencia de ancianos que está en el centro
circular una petición a los estudiantes

MODELO You hear: Soy una persona muy generosa y muy paciente. Tengo automóvil, hablo español e inglés y estudio medicina.
You write: *Puedes llevar a alguien al médico.*

1. ____.
2. ____.
3. ____.
4. ____.
5. ____.
6. ____.

Nombre: ______________________________ Fecha: ______________________

04-34 Una voluntaria.

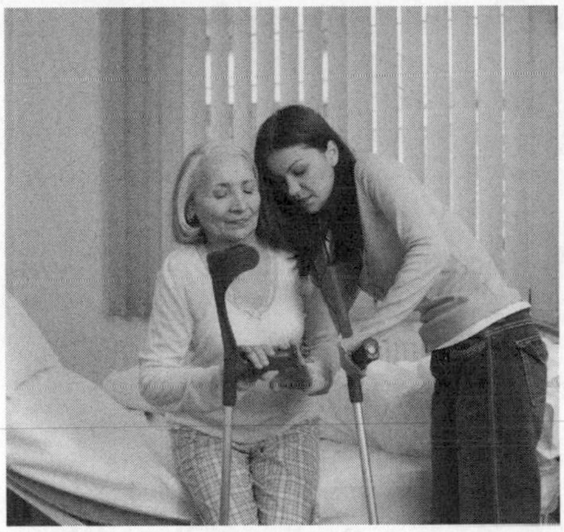

Paso 1. Look at the photograph and using the questions below to help guide you, jot down notes about the woman and what kind of volunteer work she does. Do not use complete sentences.

¿Cómo es físicamente? ¿Cómo piensas que es su personalidad? ¿Dónde está? ¿Qué hace para su comunidad? ¿Por qué piensas que ayuda a su comunidad de esa manera (*in that way*)?

____

____

____

____

Paso 2. Using your notes from **Paso 1**, describe the woman, where she is, and the kind of volunteer work she does. Explain also the kind of personality you think she must have in order to successfully do the kind of work that she does. Describe also some of the reasons why you think she chooses to do the work that she does.

Paso 3. Using your notes from **Paso 1**, compare yourself to the identity that you have imagined for the woman. What kind of personality traits do you have in common with her? What about your own personality do you think makes you a good candidate for volunteering in the context in which this woman works? Do you participate in similar volunteer activities? Why or why not?

____

____

____

____

____

____

____

04-35 Tus actividades en tu comunidad.

Paso 1. Answer the following questions about yourself and your community.

1. En tu opinión, ¿cuáles son los grupos de personas en tu comunidad que necesitan mucha ayuda?

____

2. ¿Qué ayuda y apoyo necesitan esas personas?

____

3. ¿Qué organizaciones en tu comunidad necesitan más voluntarios?

____

4. ¿Con qué grupos de personas o con qué organizaciones puedes trabajar como voluntario?

____

5. ¿Qué puedes hacer para ayudar a esas personas y esas organizaciones?

____

6. ¿Quieres trabajar como voluntario en el futuro? ¿Por qué sí o por qué no?

____

7. ¿Crees que vas a trabajar como voluntario en el futuro? ¿Por qué sí o por qué no?

____

Paso 2. Describe what you currently do or what you can do in order to serve your community. Mention also what you plan to do in the future to serve your community, and why you are going to serve in that way.

Nombre: ______________________ Fecha: ______________________

04-36 Heritage Language: *tu español*. In many parts of the Spanish-speaking world, people engage in a wide variety of activities to serve their communities. Conduct research on the specific practices of people from a specific region. If you are of Spanish-speaking heritage, interview a member of your own family. If you are not, then interview a friend, relative, or fellow student who is.

Paso 1. Use the following questions to guide you through your interview and write notes about the person's responses. Do not use complete sentences.

1. En general, ¿piensas que participan muchas personas en tu país en el voluntariado? ¿Por qué sí o por qué no?

____

____

____

2. ¿Cuáles son algunos trabajos voluntarios típicos en tu país?

____

____

3. ¿Cuáles son algunos trabajos voluntarios que piensas que tienen que hacer más personas en tu país? ¿Por qué?

____

____

____

Paso 2. Using your notes from **Paso 1**, give a brief report about your findings.

Paso 3. Using your notes from **Paso 1**, write a comparative description about the practices that the person who you interviewed described with the practices that you believe are predominant in the United States.

____

____

____

____

____

____

____

____

____

Nombre: ______________________ Fecha: ______________________

Nota cultural: La conciencia social (Textbook p. 151)

04-37 La conciencia social. Indicate if the following statements are **Cierto** or **Falso**, based on the information in your text.

1. Podemos ver mucho interés en el servicio a la comunidad en Los Estados Unidos, pero no tanto en los países hispanohablantes. Cierto Falso
2. No es posible demostrar tu interés en el servicio a la comunidad en tu trabajo si recibes un salario. Cierto Falso
3. Puedes demostrar tu conciencia social siendo (*by being*) entrenador para un equipo de fútbol de niños. Cierto Falso
4. En Los Estados Unidos hay mucha necesidad de voluntarios para ayudar a los ancianos y a los niños. Cierto Falso
5. En un trabajo para un político no es posible demostrar tu conciencia social. Cierto Falso
6. En los países hispanohablantes no hay muchos voluntarios. Cierto Falso
7. Muchos hispanos sirven a sus comunidades cuando ven que otras personas necesitan su apoyo y ayuda. Cierto Falso

Gramática

8. Las expresiones afirmativas y negativas: Articulating concepts and ideas both affirmatively and negatively (Textbook p. 151)

04-38 Diferentes tipos de estudiante. For each statement, indicate to which type of student it corresponds.

1. Siempre va a todas sus clases.
   el estudiante desastroso
   el estudiante normal
   el estudiante perfecto
2. Nunca va a sus clases.
   el estudiante desastroso
   el estudiante normal
   el estudiante perfecto
3. Normalmente va a sus clases, a veces no puede ir porque está enfermo.
   el estudiante desastroso
   el estudiante normal
   el estudiante perfecto
4. Normalmente estudia mucho para sus clases, pero a veces no estudia.
   el estudiante desastroso
   el estudiante normal
   el estudiante perfecto
5. Nunca puede estudiar porque tiene una vida social muy activa.
   el estudiante desastroso
   el estudiante normal
   el estudiante perfecto
6. Cuando tiene que hacer una presentación en grupo, nunca hace su parte.
   el estudiante desastroso
   el estudiante normal
   el estudiante perfecto
7. Cuando necesitas usar los apuntes de otra persona para estudiar, siempre prefieres usar los apuntes de esta persona porque son excelentes.
   el estudiante desastroso
   el estudiante normal
   el estudiante perfecto

04-39 En una residencia de ancianos. Complete the conversation betweeen Marta and Clara by choosing the correct affirmative or negative expression.

MARTA: Perdón, pero ¿sabes si (1) (algún / alguna / alguien) persona puede ayudar con esta parte del proyecto de artesanía?

CLARA: Lo siento, no hay (2) (nadie / ningún / ninguna) persona libre en este momento; todo el mundo (*everybody*) está muy ocupado.

MARTA: ¿Puedes ayudarme tú con (3) (algo / nada / alguno)?

CLARA: Estoy aquí para ayudar con las excursiones. No sé (4) (algo / nada / nunca) de la artesanía, no tengo (5) (algún / ningún / nada) talento para los proyectos creativos y (6) (siempre / nunca / nadie) hago cosas artísticas.

MARTA: Pero esto es muy fácil. Solamente necesito a (7) (alguien / nadie / algo) para ayudarme a pintar estos papeles de un color.

CLARA: Entonces, sí que es (8) (nada / alguna / algo) que puedo hacer. ¡Claro que te ayudo!

04-40 Heritage Language: *tu español*. As you have learned, not all affirmative and negative expressions work the same way in Spanish as their equivalent expressions in English. Sharpen your awareness of these expressions by using the correct expressions to complete the conversation between Marta, a woman who is traveling around El Salvador, and Daniel, a man from a small town that she is visiting.

ningún	nada	algunas	siempre	algún
a veces	alguna	nadie	algo	

MARTA: Hola, buenas tardes. ¿Me puede decir si hay (1) ______________ restaurante abierto ahora?

DANIEL: Lo siento, pero en este momento no hay (2) ______________ restaurante abierto; todos están cerrados.

MARTA: ¿Sabe si hay (3) ______________ tienda abierta, para comprar (4) ______________ de comer?

DANIEL: Señorita, lo siento, pero no hay (5) ______________ para hacer en este pueblo hasta (*until*) las cinco de la tarde. En este momento no hay (6) ______________ más que yo en la calle; todas las personas del pueblo están en sus casas.

MARTA: ¡Qué curioso! ¿(7) ______________ siguen este horario?

DANIEL: No, (8) ______________ en el invierno (9) ______________ personas siguen otro horario.

MARTA: Bueno, muchas gracias por su tiempo y su ayuda, y buenas tardes.

DANIEL: Adiós.

Gramática

9. Un repaso de *ser* y *estar*: Describing states of being, characteristics, and location (Textbook p. 154)

04-41 ¿Quién es y dónde está? Isabel has a very international family and group of friends. Listen to her talk about some important people in her life and then, using the expressions in the word bank, indicate what each person's relationship to her is and where each person is.

su profesor	su hermana	el novio de su hermana	su tío
su tía	su prima	en Montevideo	en México, D.F.
en Madrid	en San Francisco	en Buenos Aires	en Sevilla

	¿Quién es?	¿Dónde está?
1. Esteban		
2. Lina		
3. Silvia		
4. Rolando		
5. Arantxa		
6. Javier		

04-42 ¿Cómo son mis amigos? Ana has very diverse friends. Complete the paragraph about them using the correct forms of ***ser***.

Mis amigos (1) ______________ de diferentes países del mundo: Carolina y Pablo (2) ______________ colombianos, Jorge y yo (3) ______________ peruanos, Kiroko (4) ______________ japonesa y Stephanie y Norbert (5) ______________ alemanes. Todos nosotros (6) ______________ estudiantes muy buenos. Creo que todos mis amigos (7) ______________ inteligentes y simpáticos.

04-43 ¿Cómo están mis amigos? Some of Ana's friends are doing well, and others are not feeling very well at all. Complete the paragraph about how her friends are feeling using the correct forms of ***estar***. Be careful, not all of the items require a conjugated form of the verb.

Quiero tener una fiesta en mi casa hoy, pero creo que no va a ser posible. Carolina (1) ________________ muy estresada porque tiene dos exámenes esta semana. Jorge y Pablo van a (2) ________________ muy cansados porque tienen que jugar al fútbol esta tarde. Walter (3) ________________ muy enfermo, así que no tiene ganas de ir a una fiesta. Kiroko y su novio (4) ________________ en Nueva York para ver una exposición importante en un museo de arte, y Stephanie (5) ________________ en Boston para un concierto. Mi amigo Enrique y yo (6) ________________ muy contentos y queremos hacer una fiesta, pero creo que va a ser imposible. ¡Ahora yo (7) ________________ triste!

04-44 ¡Llegamos tarde! Alicia and Manolo are in a big hurry and need to leave in order to arrive to class on time. Complete their conversation with the correct forms of ***ser*** or ***estar***.

ALICIA: Oye, Manolo, tenemos que salir. ¿(1) ________________ preparado o necesitas más tiempo?

MANOLO: Sí, ahora salgo.

ALICIA: Oye, Manolo, ¿(2) ________________ bien?

(3) ________________ las ocho menos cuarto de la mañana y tenemos clase a las ocho en punto (*on the dot*). ¡Tienes que darte más prisa!

MANOLO: ¡Qué impaciente (4) ________________, Alicia! ¿No puedes (5) ________________ un poco más simpática?

ALICIA: ¡No, porque no quiero llegar tarde a la clase! ¿Dónde (6) ________________? ¿En tu cuarto?

MANOLO: Sí, Luis y yo (7) ________________ aquí, puedes venir si quieres.

ALICIA: ¿Qué pasa, Manolo?

MANOLO: (8) ________________ triste porque no me gusta la ropa que tengo.

ALICIA: Manolo, (9) ________________ muy guapo, por eso no es importante tu ropa. ¿Verdad, Luis?

¡Pero creo que Manolo necesita (10) ________________ más puntual!

Nombre: ______________________________ Fecha: ______________________

04-45 Heritage Language: *tu español*. Interview three friends, relatives, or fellow students of Spanish-speaking heritage. Ask each person to describe someone from the Spanish-speaking world whom they admire.

Paso 1. Write notes on the following information for each person: **nombre, nacionalidad, profesión, ubicación actual** (*current location*), **características físicas, personalidad, por qué es digno** (*worthy*) **de admiración.**

1. ____

____

2. ____

____

3. ____

____

Paso 2. Using your notes from **Paso 1**, describe the three people paying special attention to the appropriate uses and the correct forms of ***ser*** and ***estar***.

Paso 3. Using your notes from Paso 1, write a comparative description of the three people, highlighting their main similarities and differences. Be careful to use ***ser*** and ***estar*** appropriately and to conjugate them correctly.

____

____

____

____

____

____

____

____

____

Escucha (Textbook p. 157)

04-46 La vida en mi pueblo.

Paso 1. Listen to Carmen's description of life in her town, and then answer the questions. If necessary, listen more than once.

1. ¿Cuáles son tres ideas importantes que menciona Carmen?

____

2. ¿Cómo ayudan las personas en su pueblo a otras personas?

____

3. ¿Cómo son las fiestas (*major holidays*) en su pueblo?

____

Paso 2. Write three sentences explaining the main ideas of Carmen's description.

____

____

____

¡Conversemos! (Textbook p. 158)

04-47 La comunidad y el servicio a la comunidad. Review the vocabulary for **Servicios a la comunidad**. For each area mentioned in the vocabulary presentation, discuss whether or not you have experience contributing to those areas of your community in those ways. Then briefly describe your personality and the volunteer activities that you think you can do best.

Nombre: ______________________ Fecha: ______________________

Escribe (Textbook p. 159)

04-48 Tu pueblo o tu ciudad.

Paso 1. Answer the following questions about your home city or town or about the city or town where your university is located.

1. ¿Qué lugares interesantes hay en tu pueblo o en tu ciudad? ¿Cuánto cuesta ir a esos lugares?

____

____

2. ¿Cuál es tu lugar favorito del pueblo o de la ciudad? ¿Qué puedes hacer en ese lugar?

____

____

3. ¿A dónde puedes ir de excursión desde tu pueblo o tu ciudad? ¿Por qué son interesantes esos lugares? ¿Qué puedes hacer en esos lugares?

____

____

4. ¿Cuál es el mejor restaurante? ¿Qué tipo de comida sirven? ¿Cuánto cuesta la comida?

____

____

5. ¿Cuál es el mejor restaurante con comida que no cuesta mucho dinero? ¿Qué tipo de comida (china, italiana, etc.) sirven? ¿Cuánto cuesta la comida?

____

____

Paso 2. Use the information from **Paso 1** to assist you as you describe your town or city.

Paso 3. Una guía para visitantes. Now organize the information from **Paso 1** in order to create a tour guide of the town or city for visitors.

____

____

____

____

____

____

Nombre: ______________________ Fecha: ______________________

Cultura: Honduras, Guatemala, and El Salvador (Textbook pp. 161–163)

04-49 Honduras. Answer the questions about César Alfonso and Honduras using the information from your text. Give only the correct information; do not use complete sentences.

1. ¿De qué ciudad es César Alfonso?

____

2. ¿Qué grupo indígena habita Honduras desde la época precolombina?

____

3. ¿Dónde están las ruinas más importantes que tienen en Honduras?

____

4. ¿Cuál es la moneda oficial de Honduras?

____

5. ¿Cuál es el nombre original de Honduras?

____

Nombre: ______________________ Fecha: ______________________

04-50 Guatemala. Complete the following statements about Luis Pedro Aguirre Maldonado and Guatemala using the information from your text.

1. Luis Pedro es de ________________, Guatemala.
2. La geografía de Guatemala es ________________ y tiene muchos volcanes.
3. En la importante ciudad de ________________ hay ruinas mayas.
4. Unas estructuras arquitectónicas mayas interesantes que hay en Guatemala son ________________.
5. La moneda oficial de Guatemala es ________________.
6. El calendario maya tiene ________________ meses.

04-51 El Salvador. Answer the questions about Claudia Figueroa Barrios and El Salvador using the information from your text. Do not respond in complete sentences; provide only the information requested.

1. ¿Cuántas costas tiene El Salvador?

   ____

2. ¿A qué playa de El Salvador puedes ir si te gustan los deportes acuáticos?

   ____

3. ¿Cuántas generaciones viven en la casa de Claudia?

   ____

4. ¿Cuál es la moneda oficial de El Salvador?

   ____

5. ¿A quiénes van algunos salvadoreños especialmente en las zonas rurales para encontrar ayuda médica?

   ____

Nombre: ______________________________ Fecha: ______________________

04-52 Vistas culturales: Honduras. View the video segments in order to complete each part of the activity. You will likely not understand all of the words that you hear, but you should relax because you are capable of understanding more than enough to be able to respond to the questions without difficulty. Please be sure to read the questions that you will have to answer before viewing each video segment.

Paso 1. Introducción. Read the questions, skim through the possible answers, and then view the video in order to determine the correct answer for each question.

1. ¿Cuál es la población de Honduras?
   casi setenta mil personas
   casi setecientas mil personas
   casi siete millones de personas
   casi setenta millones de personas

2. ¿Cuál es la capital de Honduras?
   Honduras
   Tegucigalpa
   San Pedro Sula

3. ¿Con qué masa o masas (*body or bodies*) de agua tiene costa?
   el Mar Mediterráneo
   el Océano Pacífico
   el Mar Negro
   el Mar Caribe
   el Océano Indico

Paso 2. La cocina. Read the questions, skim through the possible answers, and then view the video in order to determine the correct answer for each question.

4. ¿Cuáles son algunas comidas (*foods*) que comen muchos hondureños?
   pasta
   frutas tropicales
   pizza

5. ¿Cuáles son las bases de la dieta hondureña?
   la tortilla de maíz (*corn*)
   el arroz (*rice*)
   los frijoles (*beans*)

6. ¿Cómo se llama el arroz con frijoles (*beans with rice*) en Honduras?
   gallo pinto
   casamiento

7. ¿Qué otros alimentos (*foods*) son partes importantes de la dieta de los hondureños?
   el plátano (*plantain*)
   el brócoli
   la yuca

Paso 3. El turismo. Read the questions, skim through the possible answers, and then view the video in order to determine the correct answer for each question.

8. ¿Qué es Copán?
   un destino turístico importante
   un lugar donde hay ruinas arqueológicas
   un lugar donde hay muchas playas
   un lugar donde hay arrecifes (*reefs*) de coral

9. ¿Qué civilización vivía en Copán?
   los españoles
   los mayas
   los roatán

10. ¿Dónde en Honduras es posible hacer deportes acuáticos?
   Copán
   Islas de la Bahía
   Isla de Roatán

04-53 Vistas culturales: Guatemala. View the video segments in order to complete each part of the activity. You will likely not understand all of the words that you hear, but you should relax because you are capable of understanding more than enough to be able to respond to the questions without difficulty. Please be sure to read the questions that you will have to answer before viewing each video segment.

Paso 1. Introducción. Read the questions, skim through the possible answers, and then view the video in order to determine the correct answer for each question.

1. ¿Cuál es la población de Guatemala?
   casi ciento veinticinco mil personas
   casi un millón doscientas cincuenta personas
   casi doce millones quinientas mil personas
   casi ciento veinticinco millones de personas

2. ¿Con qué países tiene fronteras Guatemala?
   Estados Unidos
   México
   Belice
   Honduras
   El Salvador
   Nicaragua

3. ¿Con qué masa o masas (*body or bodies*) de agua tiene costa Guatemala?
   el Mar Mediterráneo
   el Océano Pacífico
   el Mar Negro
   el Mar Caribe
   el Océano Indico

4. ¿En qué parte del país hay volcanes?
   el norte
   el sur

5. ¿En qué parte del país hay muchas plantaciones?
   el norte
   el sur

6. ¿En qué parte del país hay muchas selvas subtropicales?
   el norte
   el sur

7. ¿En qué parte del país están las ruinas mayas de Tikal?
   el norte
   el sur

Paso 2. La resistencia cultural indígena. Read the questions, skim through the possible answers, and then view the video in order to determine the correct answer for each question.

8. ¿Cuántos idiomas de origen maya se hablan en Guatemala hoy en día?
   2
   12
   21
   210

9. ¿En qué año gana Rigoberta Menchú el premio Nobel de la Paz?
   1982
   1992
   2002

10. ¿Por qué gana Rigoberta Menchú el premio Nóbel de la Paz?
    porque habla muchas lenguas indígenas
    porque lucha para los derechos de los indígenas
    porque mantiene aspectos de la cultura indígena

Paso 3. La Guatemala colonial. Read the questions, skim through the possible answers, and then view the video in order to determine the correct answer for each question.

11. ¿Cuál es el nombre original de Antigua, Guatemala?
    Ciudad de Guatemala
    Santiago de Guatemala
    Ciudad Maya

12. ¿Cuándo empieza a ser la capital de Guatemala?
    1453
    1543
    1663
    1773

13. ¿Qué atracciones turísticas tiene Antigua?
    edificios viejos
    edificios coloniales
    iglesias

14. ¿Qué podemos comprar en Antigua?
    productos de los españoles
    productos coloniales
    productos de los indígenas

15. ¿Qué semana es especialmente importante en Antigua?
    la semana del 25 de diciembre
    la semana del 1 de enero
    la Semana Santa

Nombre: ______________________________ Fecha: ________________________

04-54 Vistas culturales: El Salvador. View the video segments in order to complete each part of the activity. You will likely not understand all of the words that you hear, but you should relax because you are capable of understanding more than enough to be able to respond to the questions without difficulty. Please be sure to read the questions that you will have to answer before viewing each video segment.

Paso 1. Introducción. Read the questions, skim through the possible answers, and then view the video in order to determine the correct answer for each question.

1. ¿Cuántas personas viven en El Salvador?
   casi setenta mil personas
   casi setecientas mil personas
   casi siete millones de personas
   casi setenta millones de personas

2. ¿Cuál es la capital de El Salvador?
   El Salvador
   Tegucigalpa
   San Salvador
   San Pedro Sula

3. ¿Con qué masa o masas (*body or bodies*) de agua tiene costa El Salvador?
   el Mar Mediterráneo
   el Océano Pacífico
   el Mar Negro
   el Mar Caribe
   el Océano Indico

4. ¿Cuántos kilómetros cuadrados (*squared*) tiene El Salvador?
   2.100 210.000
   21.000 2.100.000

Paso 2. La geografía y el clima. Read the questions, skim through the possible answers, and then view the video in order to determine the correct answer for each question.

5. ¿En qué zona de Centroamérica hay muchos volcanes?
   en la zona pacífica
   en la zona central

6. ¿Cuál es la zona de Centroamérica que es buena para la agricultura?
   la zona pacífica
   la zona central

7. ¿Dónde están las montañas de Centroamérica?
   en la zona pacífica
   en la zona central

8. ¿Qué tiempo hace en El Salvador?
   Generalmente hace calor en primavera, verano y otoño.
   Generalmente hace calor en primavera y verano.
   Generalmente hace calor en otoño e invierno.
   Generalmente hace calor en primavera, verano, otoño e invierno.

9. ¿Cuándo es la época de lluvias en El Salvador?
   de noviembre a abril
   de diciembre a febrero
   de junio a agosto
   de mayo a octubre

10. ¿Cuándo es la época seca?
    de noviembre a abril
    de diciembre a febrero
    de junio a agosto
    de mayo a octubre

Paso 3. CAFTA. Read the questions, skim through the possible answers, and then view the video in order to determine the correct answer for each question.

11. ¿Qué es CAFTA?
    un Tratado de Libre Comercio con América del Sur
    un Tratado de Libre Comercio con Europa
    un Tratado de Libre Comercio con Estados Unidos

12. ¿Cuál es el objetivo de CAFTA?
    crear más relaciones económicas entre los diferentes países del tratado
    mejorar las situaciones económicas de los países de Centroamérica

Nombre: ______________________________ Fecha: ________________________

Más cultura

04-55 Los barrios. Read the information about **barrios** or neighborhoods in Spanish-speaking places, and then answer the questions using complete sentences.

- Un barrio es una parte de una ciudad o de un pueblo. En estas subdivisiones de las ciudades frecuentemente los vecinos (*neighbors*) se conocen y se sienten identificados y unidos.
- Un barrio de una ciudad normalmente tiene muchas casas o edificios de apartamentos, una iglesia y diferentes tiendas pequeñas donde la gente del barrio puede comprar comida y otras cosas necesarias.
- Muchas ciudades del mundo tienen barrios donde viven muchas personas del mismo origen étnico o nacional. Por ejemplo, en muchas grandes ciudades como Nueva York y Washington, hay barrios chinos. En Nueva York también hay un barrio puertorriqueño muy importante. En Miami, hay un barrio cubano que se llama la pequeña Habana y también hay otros barrios latinoamericanos. Con la reciente inmigración de muchos latinoamericanos a España, en muchas ciudades españolas ahora hay también barrios latinoamericanos y africanos.
- En algunas partes de algunos países, como Venezuela y Estados Unidos, la palabra "barrio" puede tener connotaciones negativas, y referirse a zonas de las ciudades donde frecuentemente hay muchos problemas de delincuencia y de crímenes.

1. ¿Qué es un barrio? ¿Existe el mismo concepto en inglés?

____

____

2. ¿Qué tiene un barrio de una ciudad, normalmente?

____

____

3. ¿Qué barrios étnicos existen en los Estados Unidos?

____

____

4. ¿En qué país hay ahora diferentes barrios étnicos y por qué tienen esos barrios ahora?

____

____

5. Cuando la palabra "barrio" tiene un significado negativo, ¿a qué tipo de subdivisión de una ciudad se refiere?

____

____

Nombre: ______________________ Fecha: ______________________

04-56 Los lugares en Estados Unidos con nombres de origen hispano. Read the text about the Spanish origin of many place names in the United States, and then answer the questions using complete sentences.

- A través de (*through*) sus nombres, muchos lugares de los Estados Unidos demuestran la herencia (*heritage*) y la presencia histórica de los hispanos en este país. Muchos lugares empiezan como parte de los territorios españoles de la época colonial y posteriormente como parte de México y, por eso, conservan hasta hoy sus nombres hispanos originales.

- Algunos lugares tienen nombres que se relacionan con sus características geográficas. Montana, por ejemplo, se llama así porque es una zona muy montañosa. Las Vegas tiene su nombre porque en la época de expansión hacia el oeste (*west*) es una zona famosa por la fertilidad de su tierra (*land*). Colorado tiene su nombre por los colores de sus paisajes (*landscapes*).

- El origen de los nombres de otros lugares de los Estados Unidos viene de la flora y fauna de la región. Así también son los casos de Alcatraz y Alameda. La Florida se llama así porque tiene muchas flores diferentes.

- Otros lugares tienen nombres que reflejan (*reflect*) las condiciones climáticas y meteorológicas de sus zonas. Nevada tiene su nombre por la nieve que cae en partes del estado. La Sierra Nevada también demuestra que esas montañas reciben mucha nieve.

- Muchos nombres de lugares fundados durante la época colonial tienen un origen religioso. Hay muchas ciudades que tienen nombres de santos (*saints*), como San Antonio, San Diego y San Francisco. Otras ciudades tienen el nombre de la Virgen María. Este es el caso del nombre de la ciudad de Los Ángeles; su nombre completo en realidad es "El Pueblo de Nuestra Señora la Reina de los Ángeles del Río de Porciúncula". El nombre de la ciudad de Sacramento también es de origen católico.

1. ¿Por qué muchos lugares de los Estados Unidos tienen nombres de origen hispano?

____

____

2. Identifica cuatro lugares en los Estados Unidos cuyos (*whose*) nombres se asocian con las características geográficas de la zona.

____

____

Nombre: ______________________ Fecha: ______________________

3. Identifica tres lugares en los Estados Unidos que tienen nombres que vienen de las plantas y los animales de esa zona.

____

____

4. Identifica dos lugares en los Estados Unidos que tienen nombres que se refieren al clima de esos lugares.

____

____

5. Identifica tres lugares en los Estados Unidos que tienen nombres de origen religioso.

____

____

6. ¿Cuál es el nombre completo de la ciudad de Los Ángeles?

____

____

Nombre: ______________________________ Fecha: ______________________

04-57 El sistema métrico. Read the text about the metric system, and then answer the questions using complete sentences.

- Como en los Estados Unidos, en todos los países del mundo hispánico las personas que trabajan en las ciencias usan el sistema métrico. Pero a diferencia de (*unlike*) los Estados Unidos, en la mayoría de estos países también usan el sistema métrico en la vida diaria (*daily*).
- Cuando hablan de las distancias largas (*long*) y cuando usan sus automóviles, las personas no hablan de millas, hablan de kilómetros. Cuando hablan de un campo de fútbol, no hablan de yardas, sino que se refieren a metros. Cuando hablan de cosas más pequeñas, no las miden (*measure*) con pies (*feet*) y pulgadas (*inches*), sino que hablan de metros y centímetros. No compran un galón de leche (*milk*) como en los Estados Unidos, sino que compran litros de leche.
- No es muy difícil hacer la conversión del sistema estadounidense al sistema métrico. Una milla es aproximadamente 1,5 kilómetros. Un metro es equivalente a una yarda y hay tres pies en un metro. Una pulgada es aproximadamente 2,5 centímetros. Hay aproximadamente cuatro litros en un galón y un kilo es un poco más de dos libras (*pounds*).

1. ¿Qué sistema de medidas (*measuring*) usan los científicos de los países hispanos y en los Estados Unidos?

____

____

2. ¿Cuántos kilómetros hay en una milla?

____

____

3. ¿Cuántos centímetros hay en una pulgada?

____

____

4. ¿Cuántos metros hay en una yarda?

____

____

5. ¿Cuántos pies hay en un metro?

____

____

6. ¿Aproximadamente cuántos kilos hay en una libra?

____

____

Nombre: ______________________ Fecha: ______________________

04-58 Heritage Language: *tu mundo hispano*. As you know, mobile phone use is extremely prevalent in the United States. Conduct research on the prevalence of mobile phones in a specific Spanish-speaking country. If you are of Spanish-speaking heritage, interview a person from your own family's country of origin. If you are not, then interview a friend, relative, or fellow-student who is.

Paso 1. Write down at least five questions that you will ask the person who you plan to interview. You could consider asking the person about how common it is for different age groups to have mobile phones, what kind of customs people have about using phones in public places and/or in cars.

____

____

____

____

____

Paso 2. Conduct the interview and write down notes about the person's responses to your questions.

____

____

____

____

Paso 3. Describe the results of your findings and how they compare to the practices that you have observed in the United States.

Ambiciones siniestras

Episodio 4

Lectura: *Las cosas no son siempre lo que parecen* (Textbook p. 164)

04-59 La lectura. Answer the questions about the episode of *Ambiciones siniestras*, using complete sentences.

1. ¿Por qué no pueden celebrar Marisol y Lupe?
   a. tienen que hacer trabajo para una clase
   b. no son finalistas
   c. tienen que terminar un proyecto de servicio a la comunidad para sus pueblos

2. ¿Cómo es el lugar donde está la casa de los padres de Lupe?
   a. tranquilo y misterioso
   b. tranquilo y con un jardín pequeño
   c. tranquilo y con un jardín grande

3. ¿A quién le gusta hablar de su familia?
   a. a Manolo
   b. a Marisol
   c. a Lupe

4. ¿Cómo es el pueblo de Marisol?
   a. tiene muchas tiendas
   b. tiene muchos árboles
   c. está en una zona rural

5. ¿Por qué tiene que salir Lupe?
   a. para ir a comprar algo en una tienda
   b. para comprar un nuevo teléfono
   c. para llamar a alguien

6. ¿Qué hace Marisol cuando sale Lupe?
   a. trabajar en su proyecto
   b. hacer una llamada por teléfono
   c. mirar el proyecto de Lupe

Video: *¿Quiénes son en realidad?* (Textbook p. 166)

04-60 ¿Quiénes somos en realidad? View the episode of *Ambiciones siniestras* and then indicate if the following statements are **Cierto** or **Falso**.

1. Cisco y Eduardo tienen que comprar cosas en el supermercado. Cierto Falso
2. Eduardo trabaja como voluntario en Centroamérica durante los inviernos. Cierto Falso
3. La organización de Eduardo ayuda a los ancianos. Cierto Falso
4. A Cisco le gusta la idea de servir a la comunidad y trabajar como voluntario. Cierto Falso
5. Eduardo quiere saber qué son los códigos que tiene Cisco. Cierto Falso
6. Eduardo cree que Cisco es arrogante. Cierto Falso

Nombre: ______________________ Fecha: ______________________

04-61 ¿Qué ocurre? View the video once again, and using the following questions as a guide, write a brief paragraph expressing your ideas about interpersonal conflicts in this episode.

¿Cuáles son algunos de los conflictos que hay entre los personajes (*characters*)? ¿Cuáles son las causas de esos conflictos? ¿Qué efectos piensas que van a tener esos conflictos en el futuro?

____

____

____

____

____

____

____

____

____

Comunidades

04-62 Experiential Learning: La inmigración. Research the most recent census figures for the United States, focusing on how many immigrants are from Honduras, Guatemala, or El Salvador. Then delve further into the immigration issue and try to discover if their reasons for coming to the United States reflect the same kinds of attitudes or desires that fuel the much larger number of immigrants from Mexico, and then write a reflection on your findings.

- How are their motives different? How are they similar?
- What types of jobs do they typically find in the United States?
- Are their socio-economic or educational backgrounds different from those of many Mexican immigrants?
- What could explain the varied motivations of such an eclectic group of Hispanic immigrants searching for a new life in the United States?

04-63 Service Learning: En la comunidad.

Paso 1: Contact your community United Way office or affiliate in order to obtain information about the basic services offered in Spanish to the local Hispanic community. It might also be helpful to communicate with the closest office of the Salvation Army, Goodwill, and/or your community's soups kitchens. You should also include child and family advocacy agencies and any social service resources that might be of help to the Hispanic population.

Paso 2: Work together as a class to collect as much information as possible, double-check the data that you gather and compile an official report in Spanish about the resources.

Paso 3: Once you have turned in this information to your professor and he/she has had time to review the documents, create an electronic newsletter to print and distribute for free throughout different parts of your community with large Hispanic populations.

¡A divertirse! La música y el cine

Comunicación I

Vocabulario

1. El mundo de la música: Discussing music (Textbook p. 172)

05-01 Artistas famosos. For each artist, select the instrument or instruments that he plays, based upon the drawings.

1. Dave Grohl toca , y .
   - la trompeta
   - la guitarra
   - la batería
   - el piano

2. Miles Davis toca  y .
   - la trompeta
   - la guitarra
   - el tambor
   - el piano

3. John Mayer toca y .
   - la trompeta
   - la guitarra
   - el piano
   - la batería

4. Louis Armstrong toca .
   - la trompeta
   - la guitarra
   - la batería
   - cl tambor

5. The Edge toca y .
   - la trompeta
   - la guitarra
   - la batería
   - el piano

6. Stevie Wonder toca , y .
   - la trompeta
   - el tambor
   - la batería
   - el piano

7. Arturo Sandoval toca y .
   - la trompeta
   - la guitarra
   - la batería
   - el piano

8. Phil Collins toca , y .
   - la trompeta
   - la guitarra
   - la batería
   - el piano

Nombre: ______________________ Fecha: ______________________

05-02 Crucigrama. Complete the crossword puzzle with the correct words, according to each definition.

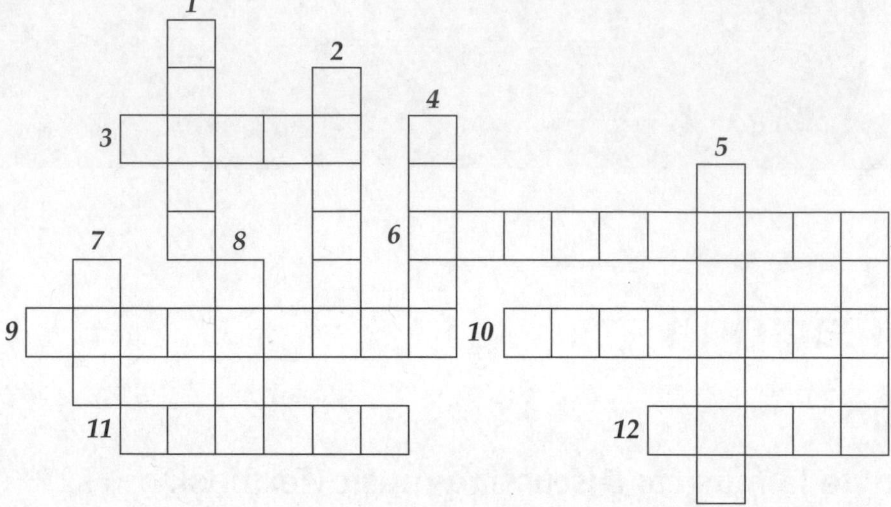

1. un género de música muy popular por todo el mundo que es similar al teatro y en el que las sopranos y los tenores son muy importantes y cantan arias
2. un instrumento de percusión que es muy importante en la música latina
3. las palabras que canta una persona en una canción
4. un instrumento muy grande que tiene teclas *(keys)* de color blanco y negro
5. lo que hacen los músicos muchas veces antes de (*before*) dar sus conciertos, para mejorar (*to improve*) sus habilidades y para poder dar buenos conciertos
6. un hombre que tiene todos los discos de un artista, que piensa que esa persona es un artista muy bueno y que quiere ir a todos sus conciertos
7. el sonido (*sound*) que produce una persona para cantar y para hablar
8. dar muchos conciertos en diferentes lugares; dar una…
9. un evento musical que puede ser grande (y tener lugar [*take place*] en un estadio), o pequeño (y tener lugar en un bar); muchas veces cuesta dinero entrar para escuchar la música
10. la persona de un grupo de música que canta las canciones
11. crear un disco de música
12. género de música latina que tiene su origen en el caribe y que es muy popular por todo el mundo, pero especialmente en lugares como Cuba, Puerto Rico y la República Dominicana

Nombre: ______________________________ Fecha: ______________________________

05-03 Los músicos del conjunto Buena Vista Social Club. Listen to the information about Buena Vista Social Club, and then, using the words provided, write what role or roles each artist plays in the group.

baterista	cantante	guitarrista	pianista	tamborista	trompetista

1. Rubén González ______________
2. Manuel "Puntillita" Licea ______________
3. Manuel "Guajiro" Mirabal ______________
4. Eliades Ochoa ______________ y ______________
5. Omara Portuondo ______________
6. Pío Leyva ______________
7. Ibrahím Ferrer ______________
8. Compay Segundo ______________
9. Joachim Cooder ______________
10. Ry Cooder ______________

05-04 Buena Vista Social Club.

Paso 1. Listen to the story of how Buena Vista Social Club was formed, and then indicate if the following affirmations are **Cierto** or **Falso**.

1. El proyecto de Buena Vista Social Club empieza en los años 80. Cierto Falso
2. El nombre "Buena Vista Social Club" se refiere a un barrio de La Habana y a un club de baile de los años 40. Cierto Falso
3. El famoso baterista cubano, Ry Cooder, empieza el proyecto. Cierto Falso
4. Cuando empiezan el proyecto, muchos de los músicos son jóvenes. Cierto Falso
5. Cuando todos los artistas empiezan a ensayar, ven que tienen muchas habilidades. Cierto Falso
6. En 1996, el conjunto saca un disco. Cierto Falso
7. En 1997, el disco recibe un premio Grammy. Cierto Falso
8. *Rolling Stone* incluye el disco en su lista de los mejores 50 discos de la historia. Cierto Falso
9. En 1999, Wim Wenders, el director norteamericano, hace un documental sobre el proyecto. Cierto Falso
10. El documental genera más de $33.000.000. Cierto Falso

Paso 2. Listen once more, and, for each false statement, rewrite the selected portions of the statement in order to make it true. For the statements that are true, leave the text as it is.

11. El proyecto de Buena Vista Social Club empieza en los años 80.
12. El nombre "Buena Vista Social Club" se refiere a un barrio de La Habana y un club de baile de los años 40.
13. El baterista cubano, Ry Cooder, empieza el proyecto.
14. Cuando empiezan el proyecto, muchos de los músicos son jóvenes.
15. Cuando todos los artistas empiezan a ensayar, ven que todavía tienen muchas habilidades.
16. En 1996, el conjunto saca un disco.
17. En 1997, el disco recibe un premio Grammy.
18. *Rolling Stone* incluye el disco en su lista de los mejores 50 discos de la historia.
19. En 1999, Wim Wenders, el director norteamericano, hace un documental sobre el proyecto.

    La película genera más de $33.000.000.

05-05 Maná. Read the following text about the rock band Maná, and then complete the statements with the correct information.

Maná es un grupo de rock y sus miembros son algunos de los artistas más populares de todo el mundo hispano. Los orígenes de la banda empiezan en los años 80, cuando unos adolescentes forman un grupo con otro nombre —"Sombrero Verde"— y deciden tocar las canciones de sus grupos de rock favoritos: los Beatles, los Rolling Stones, Led Zeppelin y The Police.

En 1987, tres de los miembros de ese grupo —Fernando Olvera y los hermanos Ulises y Juan Diego Calleros— deciden formar una nueva banda con el nombre de "Maná". En el nuevo conjunto, Olvera sigue como vocalista, Ulises Calleros continúa como guitarrista y Juan Diego Calleros sigue tocando el bajo *(bass guitar)*. Desde (*Since*) 1995, Sergio Vallín toca la guitarra en la banda.

Desde 1987, el grupo ha tenido *(has had)* mucha actividad profesional. Maná tiene ocho álbumes de canciones originales y otros tres discos con grabaciones de sus conciertos. Tienen también nueve compilaciones de sus mejores (*best*) canciones y tres discos que se llaman "Esenciales". Además tienen un DVD sobre la banda y su gira por el mundo que se titula "Acceso total". Sus discos recientes han tenido un éxito internacional muy grande.

El estilo de música de Maná es realmente singular; el conjunto hace una música de rock auténtico pero que también refleja la importancia de sus orígenes y su identidad latinos. Igualmente (*Equally*) singular es la conciencia social y ecológica del grupo, y su deseo de ayudar el mundo. La letra de muchas de sus canciones tiene un fuerte mensaje social o de protesta política. Desde 1995, apoyan la fundación ecológica "Selva Negra". Con esta fundación, el grupo financia muchos proyectos para proteger nuestro planeta.

1. El grupo que forman cuando son adolescentes se llama ________________.
2. Forman el grupo Maná en el año ________________.
3. El cantante del grupo se llama ________________.
4. El baterista se llama ________________.
5. La persona que toca la guitarra ahora se llama ________________.
6. La persona que toca el bajo se llama ________________.
7. Si quieres saber más del grupo y ver partes de sus conciertos, puedes comprar el DVD ________________.
8. La organización de protección ecológica de Maná se llama ________________.

05-06 Investiga y escucha. Use the Internet to find Maná's official website, as well as, their official YouTube channel in order to listen to some of their music and view some of their videos.

Paso 1. After hearing at least three different songs, write notes about each song, using the following guidelines.

- Título
- Ritmo (rápido, alegre, tranquilo, suave, lento, etc.)
- Estilo (rock, latino, apasionado, bailable, etc.)
- Mi parte favorita de la canción (guitarra, batería, voz, etc.)
- Mi opinión en general de la canción (Me gusta mucho; Me gusta; Es buena; No es muy buena; No me gusta; Es mala; La odio, etc.)

____

____

____

____

____

____

____

____

____

Paso 2. ¿Qué piensas de Maná? Using the information that you compiled above, describe your general opinion of the band and their music. As you speak, try to use words like **y, pero,** and **también** to lengthen your sentences and connect your ideas. Make certain to include the following information in your recording.

For each song:

- ¿Cómo es la canción?
- ¿Cómo es el ritmo?
- ¿Cómo es el estilo?
- ¿Te gusta? Si te gusta, ¿qué aspectos de la canción te gustan? Si no, ¿por qué no te gusta?

Your impressions about the band in general:

- ¿Crees que es un grupo bueno o malo? ¿Por qué?
- ¿Cómo describes su estilo de música? ¿Te gusta o no?

Nombre: ______________________________ Fecha: ______________________

05-07 Heritage Language: *tu español.*

Paso 1. Instrumentos de la música hispánica. Although instruments like the guitar, the drums, the piano, and the trumpet are commonly used in many types of Hispanic music, there are also many other instruments that are extremely important in these areas and many of them are of Hispanic origin. For each instrument, conduct research in order to determine with which country, or countries, it is associated.

1. quijongo
   Perú
   Costa Rica
   Nicaragua
   Ecuador

2. mejoranera
   Panamá
   Colombia
   Chile
   Argentina

3. txistu
   Cuba
   México
   Argentina
   España

4. rondador
   Guatemala
   Costa Rica
   Ecuador
   Nicaragua

5. cajón
   Chile
   Argentina
   Perú
   México

Paso 2. Ritmos y géneros. For many people outside of the Spanish-speaking world, some of the rhythms from these countries sound very similar; it is not uncommon for some people to hear lively Hispanic rhythms and refer to all of them as "salsa," even though salsa is only one of many genres. For each type of music, conduct research in order to determine with which of the country, or countries, listed it is associated.

6. cumbia
   Cuba
   Colombia
   España
   República Dominicana

7. chicha
   Costa Rica
   Panamá
   Argentina
   Perú

8. mambo
   República Dominicana
   España
   Cuba
   Chile

9. merengue
   República Dominicana
   Cuba
   Argentina
   México

10. bachata
    Uruguay
    Chile
    República Dominicana
    Cuba

11. tango
    Paraguay
    Uruguay
    República Dominicana
    Argentina

12. Palo de Mayo
    República Dominicana
    Panamá
    Argentina
    Nicaragua

13. vallenato
    Cuba
    Chile
    Bolivia
    Colombia

14. romantikeo
    Costa Rica
    Puerto Rico
    Cuba
    República Dominicana

15. salsa
    Cuba
    Uruguay
    Bolivia
    Chile

Nombre: ______________________________ Fecha: ______________________

Pronunciación: Diphthongs and linking (Textbook p. 173)

In Spanish, **a, e,** and **o** are what are known as *strong vowels.* The **i** and **u** are known as *weak vowels.* A **diphthong** is the combination of a strong and a weak vowel, or two weak vowels. Diphthongs are pronounced as a single syllable.

conc**ie**rto empresar**ia** grabac**io**nes p**ia**nista

When pronouncing words in Spanish, *linking* occurs. Linking is what makes spoken Spanish appear to flow and be seamless. What follows is a summary of how words are linked.

1. A **consonant** at the *end* of one word is linked to a **vowel** at the *beginning* of the next word.
   e**l a**rtista u**n a**ficionado ello**s e**nsayan

2. A **vowel** at the *end* of one word is linked to a **vowel** at the *beginning* of the next word.
   s**u** (h)**a**bilidad t**u o**rquesta nuestr**a ó**pera ell**a e**nsaya

3. **Identical consonants** (or consonant sounds) at the *end* of one word and at the *beginning* of the next word are linked.
   su**s s**abores co**n n**egro sabo**r r**ítmico vo**z s**uave

4. **Identical vowels** (or vowel sounds) at the *end* of one word and the *beginning* of the next word.
   l**a a**rtista músic**a a**pasionada l**a** (h)**a**bilidad l**a a**lfombra

05-08 Los diptongos.

Paso 1. Based on what you have learned about strong and weak vowels and how diphthongs are formed in Spanish, indicate **sí** if the word below contains a diphthong and **no** if it does not.

1. Europa sí no
2. europeo sí no
3. héroe sí no
4. canción sí no
5. teatro sí no
6. feria sí no
7. veo sí no
8. fuego sí no
9. apasionado sí no
10. poeta sí no

Paso 2. For each word that contains a diphthong, write the letters that make up the diphthong. For those that do not, write *none* in the space.

MODELO pianista *ia*

11. Europa ________________
12. europeo ________________
13. héroe ________________
14. canción ________________
15. teatro ________________
16. feria ________________
17. veo ________________
18. fuego ________________
19. apasionado ________________
20. poeta ________________

Nombre: ______________________ Fecha: ______________________

05-09 Los diptongos.

Paso 1. In each of the following words, write the vowels that according to the rules you learned could form diphthongs.

1. familia ______________
2. ciudad ______________
3. paisano ______________
4. día ______________
5. farmacia ______________
6. oigo ______________
7. contrario ______________
8. fantasía ______________
9. reino ______________
10. piano ______________

Paso 2. Los diptongos y los hiatos. Listen to each of the following words, and indicate if the diphthong is present (**diptongo**) or if the two vowels are pronounced independently (**vocables independientes**).

11. diptongo vocales independientes
12. diptongo vocales independientes
13. diptongo vocales independientes
14. diptongo vocales independientes
15. diptongo vocales independientes
16. diptongo vocales independientes
17. diptongo vocales independientes
18. diptongo vocales independientes
19. diptongo vocales independientes
20. diptongo vocales independientes

05-10 Enlaces entre palabras.

Based on what you have learned about linking between words, select **sí** if the following word combinations should be linked and **no** if they should not.

1. esta armonía sí no
2. esa canción sí no
3. aquel grupo sí no
4. este concierto sí no
5. aquella banda sí no
6. aquel conjunto sí no
7. las empresarias sí no
8. los pianistas sí no
9. los cantantes sí no
10. este género sí no

Nombre: ______________________________ Fecha: ______________________

05-11 Diptongos y enlaces.

Paso 1. For each of the sentences below, indicate the words that contain diphthongs.

1. Me encanta esta canción.
2. Ensayamos mucho antes de cada concierto.
3. Estas artistas son todas europeas.
4. En esta ciudad viven muchos aficionados a ese grupo.
5. Este es uno de los mejores pianistas del país.
6. Aquella chica va a cantar durante la feria.

Paso 2. Rewrite each of the following sentences, and indicate where linking between words could occur using dashes, as in the model.

MODELO Aquellos conjuntos son muy buenos.
Aquellos conjuntos-son muy buenos.

7. Me encanta esta canción. ______________________________.
8. Ensayamos mucho antes de cada concierto. ______________________________.
9. Estas artistas son todas europeas. ______________________________.
10. En esta ciudad viven muchos aficionados a ese grupo. ______________________________.
11. Este es uno de los mejores pianistas del país. ______________________________.
12. Aquella chica va a cantar durante la feria. ______________________________.

05-12 Los diptongos, los enlaces y la fluidez.

Practice speaking with greater fluency by pronouncing the following sentences, paying special attention to the diphthongs within the words and to the appropriate linking between the words.

1. Me encanta esta canción.
2. Ensayamos mucho antes de cada concierto.
3. Estas artistas son todas europeas.
4. En esta ciudad viven muchos aficionados a ese grupo.
5. Este es uno de los mejores pianistas del país.
6. Aquella chica va a cantar durante la feria.

Nombre: ______________________________ Fecha: ______________________

Gramática

2. Los adjetivos demostrativos: Identifying people and things (Part I) (Textbook p. 175)

05-13 ¿Qué disco compramos? Marta and Paco have a gift certificate to buy a new CD, but Marta would like to buy one CD and Paco has chosen a different one. Complete their dialogue with the correct forms of the demonstrative adjectives **este** and **ese**.

MARTA: Paco, mira, ¡tengo el disco perfecto! (1) ______________ disco es de mi grupo favorito, Fito y los Fitipaldis.

PACO: Marta, no quiero comprar (2) ______________ disco, pero me gusta mucho (3) ______________ disco que tengo yo, que es el nuevo CD de Paulina Rubio.

MARTA: No podemos comprar un disco de (4) ______________ artista. ¡No soporto (*can't stand*) (5) ______________ música!

PACO: Es evidente que tenemos que encontrar una solución. ¿Te gusta (6) ______________ música que oímos ahora, aquí en la tienda?

MARTA: Sí, me gusta mucho; creo que es Julieta Venegas. Vamos a preguntar qué disco es y vamos a comprar (7) ______________ disco.

05-14 ¿Qué discos prefiere? Carlos loves all styles and genres of music, so it is always very difficult for him to decide which CDs to listen to. Complete the sentences with the correct forms of the demonstrative adjectives **este**, **ese**, and **aquel**, based upon the drawing.

¿Qué voy a escuchar ahora? (1) ______________ disco de jazz es uno de mis favoritos, pero (2) ______________ disco de música rock también me gusta mucho. (3) ______________ disco de música clásica tiene música muy tranquila y eso es siempre bueno. Pero no, creo que prefiero escuchar (4) ______________ música jazz hoy. Más tarde puedo escuchar (5) ______________ música clásica con mi novia y por la noche podemos escuchar (6) ______________ música rock durante la fiesta.

Nombre: ______________________ Fecha: ______________________

05-15 Heritage Language: *tu español*: *Operación triunfo*. *Operación triunfo* is the Spanish equivalent of *American Idol*. Complete the following conversation between the judges about different candidates who aspire to being contestants in the show, by selecting the appropriate form of the demonstrative adjectives **este, ese,** or **aquel**. When choosing your response, note the distance between the speaker and the person or object to which they are referring; this determines that the demonstrative pronouns we use are not limited solely to physical space, but can also relate to temporal distance.

MARTA: Creo que (1) (este / aquel) chico que acaba de cantar (*has just sung*) tiene muchas habilidades. ¿Qué pensáis vosotros?

JUAN: Estoy de acuerdo, pero también pienso que (2) (esta / esa) chica rubia, de ayer por la tarde, la chica de la canción (*song*) de Shakira tiene más talento que él. ¿Y tú, Jorge, qué crees?

JORGE: Pues, creo que (3) (esta / aquella) decisión que tenemos que tomar va a ser un poco complicada. Mi candidato favorito es (4) (este / aquel) chico del viernes pasado (*last Friday*), el que cantó (*sang*) la canción de Elton John.

MARTA: ¿ (Este / Aquel) joven? ¿Estás seguro (*sure*)? En mi opinión, no tiene ningún talento y además, (6) (esta / aquella) canción demuestra que no puede cantar.

JUAN: Jorge, lo siento, pero estoy de acuerdo con Marta.

(7) (Este / Aquel) chico no es ningún artista, ¡no puede cantar! ¿Qué piensas de la rubia de ayer?

JORGE: Me gusta, creo que (8) (esta / esa) chica puede cantar bien.

MARTA: ¡Muy bien, pues, ahora tenemos una de nuestras finalistas!

Gramática

3. Los pronombres demostrativos: Identifying people and things (Part II) (Textbook p. 177)

05-16 Planes para el fin de semana. Carolina and Julieta are looking at the entertainment section of the newspaper and discussing their plans for the weekend. Listen to their conversation, and then indicate if the following statements are **Cierto** or **Falso**.

1. Julieta cree que el concierto de música árabe es una buena opción. Cierto Falso
2. A Julieta le gusta mucho la música de Los Fabulosos Cadillacs. Cierto Falso
3. Carolina piensa que Los Fabulosos Cadillacs son buenos músicos. Cierto Falso
4. El grupo Jarabe de Palo toca todos los viernes en el centro estudiantil. Cierto Falso
5. Julieta y Carolina quieren ir al concierto de Jarabe de Palo. Cierto Falso

Nombre: ______________________________ Fecha: ______________________

05-17 Heritage Language: *tu español*: Grupos de música. Read the following text about Amaral and La oreja de Van Gogh, two Spanish bands, and then indicate which nouns each demonstrative pronoun is referring to or replacing.

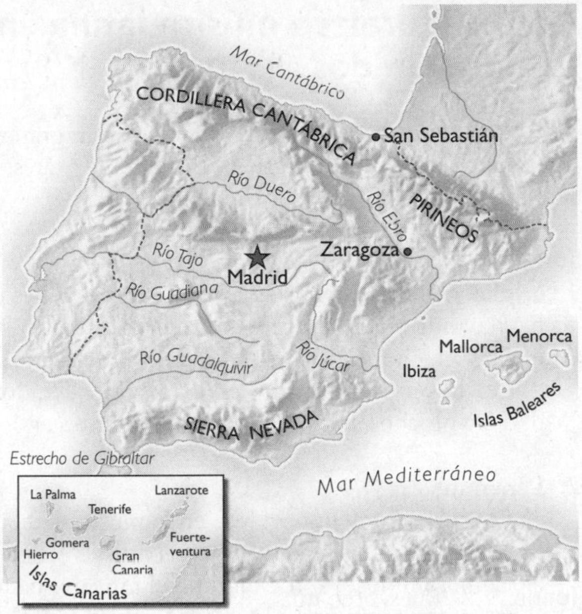

MODELO Hay muchos conjuntos de rock en España; estos[M] son muy populares con los jóvenes.

conjuntos

Amaral y La oreja de Van Gogh son dos grupos muy populares en España hoy en día. Estos[1] son dos buenos ejemplos de la música que muchos jóvenes españoles escuchan ahora. Tanto Amaral como La oreja de Van Gogh son del norte de España, este[2] de la ciudad de San Sebastián y aquel[3] de la ciudad de Zaragoza.

Los dos artistas que forman el grupo Amaral son Eva Amaral y Juan Aguirre. Este[4] tiene mucha experiencia como guitarrista, y su compañera tiene experiencia como cantante y baterista. Las canciones que escriben son diversas. En estas[5] son evidentes diferentes influencias musicales que van desde el rock tradicional hasta la música psicodélica.

Los integrantes (*members*) originales de La oreja de Van Gogh son Amaia Montero, Pablo Menegras, Xabi San Martín, Álvaro Fuentes y Haritz Garde. Estos[6] son amigos de la universidad que deciden empezar a tocar sus canciones favoritas. Rápidamente empiezan a escribir sus propias (*own*) canciones originales, todas con una letra muy singular. Esta[7] explora el mundo de la juventud y de las primeras experiencias con el amor y con el desamor. En 2007, Amaia Montero decide separarse de sus compañeros. Estos[8] empiezan inmediatamente a buscar una nueva cantante y después de poco tiempo encuentran a Leire Martínez.

1. ______________________________ 5. ______________________________

2. ______________________________ 6. ______________________________

3. ______________________________ 7. ______________________________

4. ______________________________ 8. ______________________________

Nombre: ______________________________ Fecha: ______________________________

Nota cultural: La música latina en los Estados Unidos (Textbook p. 178)

05-18 La música latina I. For each paragraph of the reading in your textbook on Latin music in the United States, select the letter of the sentence that best describes the main idea.

1. Paragraph 1:
   a. Hay géneros de música latina muy populares en los Estados Unidos.
   b. Hay muchos intérpretes de música latina en los Estados Unidos.
   c. Hay muchos tipos (*types*) diferentes de música latina y también hay muchos músicos latinos en los Estados Unidos.
   d. Hay muchos artistas latinos importantes en los Estados Unidos.

2. Paragraph 2:
   a. El rock es muy importante en la música latina en los Estados Unidos.
   b. El jazz es muy importante en la música latina en los Estados Unidos.
   c. El merenhouse, el rock latino, el rap en español, el jazz latino, el reggaetón y otros son tipos de música latina muy importantes en los Estados Unidos.
   d. Muchos nuevos tipos de música latina son el resultado de la evolución de la música latina.

3. Paragraph 3:
   a. Los países hispanohablantes tienen mucha influencia en la música latina.
   b. Los países caribeños hispanohablantes tienen mucha influencia en la música latina.
   c. La herencia africana de los países hispanohablantes tiene mucha influencia en la música latina.
   d. Los hispanohablantes y los africanos forman parte de los ritmos, las melodías y la instrumentación de la música latina.

4. Paragraph 4:
   a. Néstor Torres es un artista importante que tiene mucho éxito.
   b. Néstor Torres es un flautista de jazz latino, ganador de un Grammy latino.
   c. Hay muchos artistas de hoy en día que ganan premios importantes.
   d. La música latina en los Estados Unidos va a tener mucho éxito en el futuro.

Nombre: ______________________ Fecha: ______________________

05-19 La música latina II.

Paso 1. Answer the following questions about the important details in the reading in your textbook.

1. Identifica tres géneros de música latina que son populares en los Estados Unidos.

   ____

2. Identifica cuatro artistas que son representativos de estos géneros que el texto menciona.

   ____

3. Identifica cinco nuevos géneros de música latina que demuestran la influencia de otros géneros musicales.

   ____

4. ¿En qué aspectos de la música latina influyen los países del Caribe?

   ____

5. ¿Qué género de música toca Néstor Torres?

   ____

Paso 2. ¿Qué piensas tú? Based on what you have learned about different types of Latin music, briefly describe which genres you might want to learn more about and which ones you would not like to listen to, and explain the reasons for your preferences. As you speak, try to use words like **y, pero,** and **también** to lengthen your sentences and connect your ideas.

MODELO *Pienso que el jazz latino tiene que ser muy interesante porque me gusta mucho el jazz. Prefiero no escuchar el rap en español porque no me gusta el rap en inglés…*

Nombre: ______________________ Fecha: ______________________

Gramática

4. Los adverbios: Explaining how something is done (Textbook p. 179)

05-20 Opuestos. Match each word to its opposite.

1. rápidamente ________ a. difícilmente
2. fácilmente ________ b. tristemente
3. fuertemente ________ c. lentamente
4. nerviosamente ________ d. débilmente
5. felizmente ________ e. horriblemente
6. perfectamente ________ f. tranquilamente

05-21 ¿Cómo lo hacen? Complete the following sentences with the most appropriate adverb.

horriblemente	fácilmente	apasionadamente	constantemente
perfectamente	lentamente	pacientemente	

1. La cantante del grupo canta algunas partes de la canción muy rápidamente. Ella necesita cantar esas partes más ________________.
2. El guitarrista no tiene talento. Toca la guitarra ________________.
3. Los artistas ensayan todos los días y saben todas las canciones. Tocan las canciones ________________.
4. El profesor de piano tiene muchos años de experiencia, sabe que no es fácil aprender a tocar un instrumento y entiende que todos cometemos errores mientras (*make mistakes while*) aprendemos. Enseña a sus estudiantes ________________.
5. El trompetista está muy motivado porque quiere tener mucho éxito en su profesión. Ensaya ________________.
6. Es una canción muy simple. Ella toca la canción ________________.
7. Canta una canción de amor a su novio. Ella canta la canción ________________.

05-22 ¿Qué piensas? Use the Internet to find the official websites and YouTube channels of both Shakira and Juanes, in order to listen to some of their music and view some of their videos.

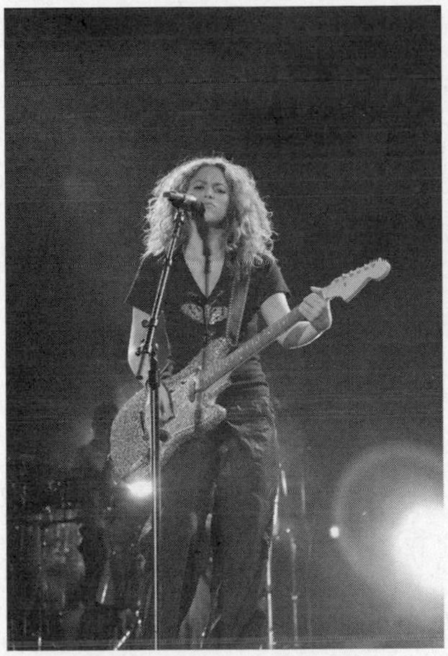

Paso 1. Using the following questions as a guide, write down some notes about your impressions of the music and talents of these two artists. Be sure to use adverbs in your notes and avoid repeating them.

- ¿Cómo piensas que cantan?
- ¿Cómo piensas que bailan?
- ¿Cómo piensas que hablan español?
- ¿Cómo piensas que hablan inglés?
- ¿Cómo piensas que tocan la guitarra?
- ¿Cómo piensas que dan conciertos?

____

____

____

____

____

____

Paso 2. Describe comparatively your impressions of these two artists, making an effort to be as descriptive as possible by using as many adverbs as possible and also being careful to use the correct forms of the verbs. As you speak, try to use words like **y, pero,** and **también** to lengthen your sentences and connect your ideas.

05-23 Heritage Language: *tu español*. Because all adverbs in Spanish ending in *-mente* have at least three syllables, for many people it can be difficult to remember to include the accent in the adverbs that require them.

Paso 1. For each adjective that you hear indicate if it requires a written accent or not by writing the word and, where relevant, placing the accent over the correct letter.

1. ______________
2. ______________
3. ______________
4. ______________
5. ______________
6. ______________
7. ______________

Paso 2. Now create the adverb for each of the adjectives listed above, being careful to include the written accent where necessary. Write the words in the same order as above.

8. ______________________
9. ______________________
10. ______________________
11. ______________________
12. ______________________
13. ______________________
14. ______________________

Gramática

5. El presente progresivo: Describing what is happening at the moment (Textbook p. 180)

05-24 ¿Qué está pasando? For each person and place, create a description of where each person is and what each person is likely doing. Complete the sentences using the present progressive form and the correct phrase from the word bank. Be sure to write the location first, and then the action, as in the model.

MODELO Tú / la oficina de correos
Estás en la oficina de correos y *estás mandando unas cartas*.

ver una película	~~mandar unas cartas~~	sacar dinero del cajero automático
escribir mensajes de correo electrónico	preparar el almuerzo	dar un concierto
jugar al básquetbol	leer un libro	

1. Marta / el banco.

   ______________________ y ______________________.

2. Julián y sus amigos / el gimnasio

   ______________________ y ______________________.

3. Yo / la biblioteca

   ______________________ y ______________________.

4. Tú / la cocina

   ______________________ y ______________________.

5. Mis amigos y yo / el cine

   ______________________ y ______________________.

6. Mario / el cibercafé

   ______________________ y ______________________.

7. Susana y su conjunto / el teatro

   ______________________ y ______________________.

Nombre: ________________________________ Fecha: ________________________

05-25 ¿Qué están haciendo? For each situation, indicate what the person is doing. Write complete sentences using the present progressive form and the correct phrase from the word bank. Follow the model closely.

grabar un disco	servir la comida	~~comprar sus libros~~	hacer una gira
dar un concierto	tocar la guitarra	almorzar	

MODELO Elena está en la librería durante la primera semana de clase en la universidad.
Está comprando sus libros.

1. Mario está en el restaurante donde trabaja. Está cerca de (*near*) una mesa donde hay clientes y tiene platos en la mano.

   ____.

2. Paco y Javier están en su restaurante favorito y tienen comida.

   ____.

3. Beyoncé está en un estadio muy grande en frente de miles de personas.

   ____.

4. Están algunos músicos en un estudio de grabación.

   ____.

5. Mario está en su casa y tiene un instrumento de música en las manos.

   ____.

6. Un conjunto toca en una ciudad diferente todas las noches.

   ____.

05-26 ¿Qué están haciendo? You are in the following places and situations. Indicate what you and your friends are probably doing.

MODELO Tus amigos y tú están en el centro comercial.
Si (if) mis amigos y yo estamos en el centro comercial, probablemente estamos comprando nuestros CD y DVD favoritos.

1. Estás en un restaurante con muchos amigos.
2. Estás con tus amigos en el garaje de tu casa y todas las personas tienen un instrumento de música.
3. Estás en el aparcamiento (*parking lot*) de un estadio y tu grupo de música favorito va a dar un concierto.
4. Tú y tus amigos tienen una banda de música y tocan para muchas personas en diferentes ciudades.
5. Estás en una discoteca y también está tu músico/a favorito/a en la discoteca.

05-27 Heritage Language: *tu español*. Because linking occurs when pronouncing words in Spanish, some combinations of words can sound exactly or almost exactly the same. As a result, it can at times be difficult to write these expressions or to know which of them has been said. For example, "**está siendo**" and "**está haciendo**" can easily be confused. Listen to each sentence and use the context to determine which of the two expressions the speaker is using.

1. está siendo   está haciendo
2. está siendo   está haciendo
3. está siendo   está haciendo
4. está siendo   está haciendo
5. está siendo   está haciendo

Comunicación II

Vocabulario

6. El mundo del cine: Sharing information about movies and television programs
(Textbook p. 184)

05-28 Películas y géneros. Look at the list of movies, and then match each film with its correct genre.

1. *Saw* ______	a. película de misterio
2. *Mamma Mia!* ______	b. película de acción
3. *Super Size Me* ______	c. película musical
4. *Sherlock Holmes 2* ______	d. película de guerra
5. *Killer Elite* ______	e. película dramática
6. *The King's Speech* ______	f. película de terror
7. *Jack and Jill* ______	g. película de humor
8. *The Hurt Locker* ______	h. película documental

Nombre: ______________________________ Fecha: ______________________

05-29 En el videoclub. You are with some friends who do not know very much about movies and they all need the help of your expertise and recommendations. For each person, choose the film that they will most likely enjoy.

1. Me gustan mucho las películas románticas. ¿Cuál de estas películas piensas que voy a preferir?
   a. *City of God*
   b. *Charlie and the Chocolate Factory*
   c. *School of Rock*
   d. *Spanglish*

2. Me encantan las películas de acción. ¿Cuál de estas películas piensas que voy a preferir?
   a. *Love Actually*
   b. *Pirates of the Caribbean 4*
   c. *The Rite*
   d. *Despicable Me*

3. Quiero divertirme y reírme (*laugh*) esta noche y no quiero pensar en cosas serias. ¿Qué película piensas que tengo que sacar?
   a. *Inception*
   b. *Contagion*
   c. *The Thing*
   d. *Jack and Jill*

4. Me encantan los automóviles y quiero divertirme esta noche con una película con mucha acción. ¿Qué película recomiendas?
   a. *The Fast and the Furious 5*
   b. *Hugo Cabret*
   c. *The Descendents*
   d. *Coriolanus*

5. También me gustan las películas de acción, especialmente las películas con elementos de ciencia ficción. ¿Qué película me recomiendas?
   a. *The Girl with the Dragon Tattoo*
   b. *We Bought a Zoo*
   c. *Brave New World*
   d. *War Horse*

6. Quiero ver una buena película dramática.
   a. *Ghostbusters 3*
   b. *Night at the Museum 3*
   c. *Johnny English 2*
   d. *Breaking Dawn*

7. Me gustan las películas de terror. ¿Qué película recomiendas?
   a. *11-11-11*
   b. *The Conspirator*
   c. *Jack and Jill*
   d. *No Strings Attached*

8. Me gusta mucho la historia y quiero ver una buena película dramática esta noche. ¿Qué película recomiendas?
   a. *Big Year*
   b. *The Mechanic*
   c. *Trespass*
   d. *J. Edgar*

05-30 ¿Qué piensas de las películas? Rate some of the films you have seen recently, and give your opinion for each of the following questions.

MODELO ¿Cuál es la mejor película dramática?
Pienso que la mejor película dramática es Infiltrados.
¿Qué película dramática te gusta más?
De las películas dramáticas, me gusta más Infiltrados.

1. ¿Cuál es la mejor película de humor?
2. ¿Qué película romántica te gusta más?
3. ¿Qué película documental te gusta más?
4. En tu opinión, ¿cuál es la mejor película de acción?
5. ¿Cuáles son algunas películas que no te gustan mucho?
6. ¿Cuál es tu película favorita?

5-31 Heritage Language: *tu español*. In addition to the words that you have learned in this chapter, there are many other terms used throughout the Spanish-speaking world associated with the film industry and the practice of movie-going. Research each of the following terms in order to determine which of the meanings corresponds to it.

1. espectadores ______________
2. butaca ______________
3. taquilla ______________
4. rodaje ______________
5. reparto ______________

a. lugar donde una persona puede comprar entradas para una película
b. los actores que están actuando en una película
c. el mueble donde una persona se sienta dentro del cine
d. grabar una película
e. la gente que está viendo una película

Nota cultural: La influencia hispana en el cine norteamericano

(Textbook p. 186)

05-32 Los actores hispanos. Based on the information in the reading in your textbook, select the Hispanic actors belonging to each category.

1. Actores hispanos importantes durante los años 50:
   America Ferrera
   Andy García
   Salma Hayek
   Diego Luna
   Ricardo Montalbán
   Anthony Quinn
   Gilbert Roland

2. Actores hispanos importantes después de los años 50:
   Antonio Banderas
   Javier Bardem
   John Leguizamo
   Jennifer López
   Rita Moreno
   Edward James Olmos
   Raquel Welch

3. Actores hispanos importantes de ahora:
   Javier Bardem
   Penélope Cruz
   America Ferrera
   Salma Hayek
   Rita Moreno
   Zoe Saldana
   Benicio del Toro

05-33 La influencia hispana en el cine norteamericano.

Paso 1. Based on the information in the reading and using your own words, write the main idea of the passage.

____

____

Paso 2. Indicate who you think are the three most influential, important, or talented Hispanic actors today, describe each of them, and mention at least one film in which each has acted.

Gramática

7. Los números ordinales: Ranking people and things (Textbook p. 187)

05-34 El Teatro Nacional Rubén Darío. You are with a friend visiting the *Teatro Nacional Rubén Darío*. Tell your friend what is happening by completing the sentences, as in the model. Remember that in Spanish the ground floor of a building is the **planta baja** and the floor immediately above that one is the **primer piso**.

MODELO Las personas que están en la planta baja <u>*dan un concierto*</u>.

1. Las personas que están en el primer piso ______________________.
2. Las personas que están en el segundo piso ______________________.
3. El tamborista está ______________________.
4. El baterista está ______________________.
5. El estudio de grabación está ______________________.
6. El estudio de ensayo está ______________________.
7. La sala de conciertos está ______________________.

05-35 Alejandro Amenábar en el cine y la música. Listen to the following report about the accomplishments of Alejandro Amenábar, the Spanish-Chilean screenwriter, director, and composer. Based on what you hear, place the following films in the correct category and in order.

1. Largometrajes (*Feature-length films*) para las que es el director:
   Tesis
   La lengua de las mariposas
   Abre los ojos
   The Others
   Nadie conoce a nadie
   Mar adentro
   Ágora

2. Películas que hace en inglés:
   The Others
   Abre los ojos
   Ágora
   Mar adentro

3. Largometrajes (*Feature-length films*) para los que escribe la música:
   Tesis
   Abre los ojos
   La lengua de las mariposas
   Nadie conoce a nadie
   The Others
   Mar adentro
   Ágora

Nombre: ______________________________ Fecha: ______________________

05-36 Las diez mejores. Do you love films? Do you adore music? Choose the one you feel most passionately about.

Paso 1. Write your top ten films or songs of all time.

1. ______________________ 6. ______________________
2. ______________________ 7. ______________________
3. ______________________ 8. ______________________
4. ______________________ 9. ______________________
5. ______________________ 10. ______________________

Paso 2. Now give your list, using ordinal numbers.

MODELO *La primera película en mi lista es* Matrix. *Mi segunda película es* Infiltrados. *La tercera película en mi lista es…*

La primera canción en mi lista es "Imagine". La segunda es "Like a Rolling Stone" y la tercera es "Smells Like Teen Spirit". Mi cuarta canción es…

05-37 Heritage Language: *tu español*. In this chapter you have learned the ordinal numbers up to ten. Ordinal numbers above ten can be challenging in Spanish. Nonetheless, because of your knowledge of numbers in Spanish, you are capable of deciphering the meaning of many of those higher ordinal numbers. For each word you hear, use your general knowledge about numbers in Spanish to determine to which number it corresponds.

1. ______ a. 50
2. ______ b. 80
3. ______ c. 30
4. ______ d. 100
5. ______ e. 60
6. ______ f. 40

Nombre: ______________________________ Fecha: ______________________

Gramática

8. *Hay que* + infinitivo: Stating what needs to be accomplished (Textbook p. 188)

05-38 ¿Cuál es tu secreto? Your friends are having some problems which you, being so balanced and level-headed, do not have to deal with. As a result they need your advice. For each problem, use the expression ***hay que*** and the appropriate verb in the infinitive to help your friends improve their situations. Be sure to use the phrases in the word bank.

buscar tiempo para descansar todos los días
estudiar un poco todos los días, comer bien, dormir bien y hacer ejercicio
hablar con los profesores o buscar un buen tutor
organizar los papeles y las tareas
~~salir con los amigos cuando invitan a personas que no conoces~~
hablar con las personas importantes en tu vida y buscar soluciones

MODELO Soy una persona bastante tímida y es muy difícil para mí conocer a gente.
Hay que salir con los amigos cuando invitan a personas que no conoces.

1. No entiendo nada en mi clase de microeconomía. La clase es difícil, pero creo que soy inteligente y que puedo entender los conceptos —¡pero no sé cómo!

   ____.

2. No saco buenas notas porque muchas veces completo mis proyectos tarde y nunca puedo encontrar nada —¡siempre lo pierdo todo!

   ____.

3. Estoy muy estresado porque tengo muchos exámenes. Otros estudiantes tienen exámenes también y no están tan (*so*) estresados.

   ____.

4. Estoy muy triste porque siempre tengo problemas con mi novio. Otras parejas nunca tienen todos los problemas que tenemos nosotros.

   ____.

5. No estoy bien porque nunca tengo tiempo para descansar, solamente (*only*) trabajo y estudio. Sé que otros estudiantes también trabajan y estudian como yo, pero ellos no están tan cansados.

   ____.

Nombre: ______________________________ Fecha: ______________________

05-39 ¿Qué hay que hacer? In order to reach certain goals, one must do certain things. Listen to each question, and then describe your strategy for reaching the goal in question, using expressions with ***hay que* + infinitivo.**

MODELO Para ganar (*to win*) la lotería, ¿qué hay que hacer?

Para ganar la lotería, hay que tener mucha suerte. / Para ganar la lotería, hay que comprar cupones de la lotería.

1. ______________________________
2. ______________________________
3. ______________________________
4. ______________________________
5. ______________________________
6. ______________________________

05-40 Heritage Language: *tu español*. The meaning of ***hay que*** is extremely different from the exclamation ***¡Ay, qué…!*** (used to express emotional reactions, both positive and negative). However, because the two expressions are pronounced exactly the same way, these words are sometimes confused in writing them. Listen to each sentence, and use the context to determine which of the two expressions are being used.

1. hay que ay, qué
2. hay que ay, qué
3. hay que ay, qué
4. hay que ay, qué

Nombre: ______________________________ Fecha: ______________________

Gramática

9. Los pronombres de complemento directo y la "a" personal: Expressing *what* or *whom* (Textbook p. 189)

05-41 ¿A qué se refiere? Yolanda and her friends are planning to see a movie this weekend, and they have invited one of your friends to go with them. Your friend is having difficulty understanding Yolanda's e-mail and needs your help. Read the message, and then indicate what each direct object pronoun is referring to. Follow the model closely.

Hola Karen:

El viernes todos mis amigos y yo vamos a ver la nueva película de acción con mi actor favorito. La[M] estrenan este fin de semana en el cine que está cerca de la universidad —aquel que tiene quince salas diferentes. ¿Lo[1] conoces? Yo tengo las entradas para mí y para mi novio porque las[2] venden en el Internet. Puedes comprar entradas para ti y para tus amigos así; si necesitas mi ayuda para comprarlas[3], te la[4] doy encantada.

Bueno, eso es todo, de momento. Si tienes preguntas, estoy aquí —solamente tienes que escribirlas[5] en un mensaje de correo electrónico para mí— ya sabes que lo[6] voy a contestar muy rápidamente porque siempre estoy conectada.

Un abrazo,
Yolanda

MODELO El viernes todos mis amigos y yo vamos a ver la nueva película de acción con mi actor favorito. La[M] estrenan este fin de semana en el cine que está cerca de la universidad —aquel que tiene quince salas diferentes.
<u>*la nueva película de acción*</u>

1. ______________________________
2. ______________________________
3. ______________________________
4. ______________________________
5. ______________________________
6. ______________________________

Nombre: ______________________ Fecha: ______________________

05-42 En el cine. Read Yolanda's message to your friend Karen in order to answer the following questions. In your responses, omit the direct objects and use the correct direct object pronouns in order to avoid unnecessary repetition, as in the model.

Hola Karen:

El viernes todos mis amigos y yo vamos a ver la nueva película de acción con mi actor favorito. La[1] estrenan este fin de semana en el cine que está cerca de la universidad —aquel que tiene quince salas diferentes. ¿Lo[2] conoces? Yo tengo las entradas para mí y para mi novio porque las[3] venden en el Internet. Puedes comprar entradas para ti y para tus amigos así; si necesitas mi ayuda para comprarlas[4], te la[5] doy encantada.

Bueno, eso es todo, de momento. Si tienes preguntas, estoy aquí —solamente tienes que escribirlas[6] en un mensaje de correo electrónico para mí—ya sabes que lo[7] voy a contestar muy rápidamente porque siempre estoy conectada.

Un abrazo,
Yolanda

MODELO ¿Van a ver la nueva película de acción Yolanda y sus amigos?
Sí, la van a ver.

1. ¿Estrenan los cines la película este fin de semana?

   ____

2. ¿Tiene el cine que está cerca de la universidad quince salas diferentes?

   ____

3. ¿Tiene Yolanda dos entradas para la película?

   ____

4. ¿Puedes comprar las entradas en el Internet?

   ____

5. ¿Mira el correo electrónico muy frecuentemente Yolanda?

   ____

Nombre: ______________________ Fecha: ______________________

05-43 Heritage Language: *tu español*. Listen to the questions about important people in the recording and film industries in the Spanish-speaking world, and then answer each question using the appropriate direct object pronoun and the correct form of the verb. If you do not know the correct answer, then conduct research online in order to determine it.

MODELO ¿Graba discos Arturo Sandoval?
Sí, los graba.
¿Toca la guitarra Arturo Sandoval?
No, no la toca.

1. ______________________.
2. ______________________.
3. ______________________.
4. ______________________.
5. ______________________.
6. ______________________.
7. ______________________.
8. ______________________.
9. ______________________.
10. ______________________.

Escucha (Textbook p. 192)

05-44 Antes de escuchar. Look at the photo, and then answer the questions.

1. ¿Cuántas personas hay en la foto?
   tres
   cuatro
   cinco
   seis
2. ¿Qué relación crees que hay entre los jóvenes?
   Son una familia.
   Son amigos.
   No se conocen. (*They do not know each other.*)
3. ¿Dónde están?
   Están en el cine.
   Están en una tienda.
   Están en un concierto.
   Están en un videoclub.
4. ¿Qué tienen?
   un DVD
   entradas para ver una película
   un CD
   entradas para un concierto
5. ¿Qué hacen los jóvenes?
   Miran sus entradas.
   Compran sus entradas.
   Venden entradas.
6. ¿En qué momento del día están?
   la tarde
   la noche
   la medianoche
7. ¿Cómo están los jóvenes?
   aburridos
   tristes
   contentos
   preocupados

05-45 Al escuchar. Read the following statements, listen to the conversation and then try to figure out the gist of what the speakers are saying. Then, listen again and indicate if the following affirmations are **Cierto** or **Falso.**

1. Los jóvenes quieren ver una película que el cine estrena hoy. Cierto Falso
2. Muchas personas quieren ver la película a la 1:00 de la tarde. Cierto Falso
3. Para recibir un descuento especial del cine hay que demostrar que eres estudiante con un documento. Cierto Falso
4. Los jóvenes tienen clase mañana. Cierto Falso
5. Los jóvenes reciben el descuento al final. Cierto Falso

05-46 Después de escuchar. Read the statements below, listen to the conversation and then complete the following statements based on what the people say.

1. Los jóvenes quieren ver la película a la(s) ________________.
   13:00
   14:00
   15:00
   16:00
2. Los jóvenes son ________________.
   estudiantes
   descuentos
   carnets
   identidades
3. Los jóvenes no pueden ________________.
   llamar a sus padres
   comprar entradas
   ver la película
   demostrar que son estudiantes
4. La señora piensa que los jóvenes son ________________.
   guapos
   estudiantes
   honestos
   simpáticos
5. Los jóvenes tienen que pagar ________________.
   $13,00
   $14,00
   $15,00
   $17,00

¡Conversemos! (Textbook p. 193)

05-47 La música y el cine. You have been invited to participate in a cultural event organized by your campus Spanish club. They need your help promoting music and film from the Spanish-speaking world.

Paso 1. La música latina. The club needs your help in a presentation about Hispanic music and musicians. Choose two musicians from the Spanish-speaking world that you have learned about in this chapter or with whom you are familiar. Discuss their talents, recordings, songs, style of music, and accomplishments.

Paso 2. Los actores hispánicos. The club needs your help in an event focused on the Hispanic presence in the U.S. and international film industries. Choose two actors from the Spanish-speaking world and describe their physical characteristics, country of origin (or familial origin), kinds of films in which they have participated, at least two specific titles of films they acted in, and any important talents or accomplishments.

Nombre: ______________________________ Fecha: ______________________

Escribe (Textbook p. 194)

05-48 Una reseña de un disco. You and a friend from class will discuss a favorite CD. Note that you'll need to work with this classmate to complete **Paso 3**.

Paso 1. Think of a CD that you particularly like. Answer the following questions about the CD.

1. ¿Cómo se llama el artista / el grupo?

   ____

2. ¿Es su primer disco? ¿el segundo? ¿el tercero?

   ____

3. ¿Cómo se llama el disco?

   ____

4. ¿Qué estilo de música es?

   ____

5. ¿Qué temas (*themes/subjects*) hay en la letra de las canciones?

   ____

   ____

6. ¿Cuántas canciones tiene?

   ____

7. ¿Cuáles son las mejores canciones?

   ____

   ____

8. ¿A quiénes les va a gustar este disco? ¿A quiénes no les va a gustar? ¿Por qué?

   ____

   ____

Paso 2. Now organize the information above into a paragraph-length review of the CD.

9. ____

   ____

   ____

   ____

   ____

   ____

Nombre: ______________________ Fecha: ______________________

Paso 3. Meet with a classmate in order to share your work, and give each other feedback and constructive criticism. Make certain to provide comments not only on each others' use of grammar and vocabulary, but also on the way that you have organized and structured your review and on the content of the messages that you communicate. Write a summary of the feedback that your classmate has provided for you.

10. ____

____

____

____

____

____

Cultura: Nicaragua, Costa Rica, and Panama (Textbook pp. 195–197)

05-49 Nicaragua.

Paso 1. Les presento mi país. Read the following statements and, based on the information in your textbook, decide whether or not they convey correct information. Rewrite the selected portions of the incorrect statements in order to make them true. If they are correct, then leave the statement as is.

1. En Nicaragua <u>no hay</u> muchos lagos.
2. En Nicaragua <u>hay</u> muchos volcanes.
3. San Cristóbal es el volcán <u>más activo</u> de Nicaragua.
4. <u>La Concha</u> es el nombre de un lago en Nicaragua.
5. Miskito es <u>una lengua oficial</u> de Nicaragua.

Paso 2. Vistas culturales. View the video segments in order to complete each part of the activity. You will likely not understand all of the words that you hear, but you should relax because you are capable of understanding more than enough to be able to respond to the questions without difficulty. Please be sure to read the questions that you will have to answer before viewing each video segment.

Nicaragua: Introducción. Read the questions, view the video and then choose the correct response to each question.

6. ¿Cuántos habitantes tiene Nicaragua?
   más de 5.000.000
   más de 500.000
   más de 50.000.000

7. ¿Cuántas costas (*coasts*) tiene?
   una
   dos
   tres

8. ¿De cuántos kilómetros cuadrados (km^2) es, aproximadamente, Nicaragua?
   13.000.000
   1.300.000
   130.000

Nicaragua: Geografía y clima. Read the questions, view the video, and then choose the correct response to each question.

9. ¿En qué región de Nicaragua hay muchos volcanes?
   en la costa del Océano Pacífico
   en la zona central
   en la costa del Mar Caribe

10. ¿En qué región hay muchas montañas?
    en la costa del Océano Pacífico
    en la zona central
    en la costa del Mar Caribe

11. ¿En qué región hay muchas selvas tropicales (*rain forests*)?
    en la costa del Océano Pacífico
    en la zona central
    en la costa del Océano Atlántico

12. ¿Qué tiempo hace normalmente en Nicaragua?
    Hace mucho frío.
    Hace calor.
    Nieva mucho.

13. ¿Durante qué meses llueve mucho en Nicaragua?
    de noviembre a abril
    de mayo a octubre
    de septiembre a noviembre

Nicaragua: Turismo. Read the questions, view the video, and then choose the correct response or responses to each question.

14. ¿Por qué es importante e interesante el lago (*lake*) Cocibolca?
    Es el segundo lago más grande (*second largest*) de América Latina.
    Es el tercer lago más grande (*third largest*) de América Latina.
    Tiene langostas (*lobsters*) de agua dulce (*fresh water*).
    Tiene tiburones (*sharks*) de agua dulce.

15. ¿Cuántas islas tiene el Archipiélago del Lago Cocibolca?
    350
    370
    360

16. ¿Qué son "Concepción" y "Maderas"?
    islas
    lagos
    volcanes

Nombre: ______________________________ Fecha: ______________________

05-50 Costa Rica.

Paso 1. Les presento mi país. Read the following statements and, based on the information in your textbook, decide whether or not they convey correct information. Rewrite the selected portions of the incorrect statements in order to make them true. If they are correct, then leave the statement as is.

1. Guaitil es <u>un parque nacional</u> en Costa Rica.
2. Sarchí es <u>un símbolo nacional</u> muy famoso por su artesanía.
3. La carreta es <u>un pueblo muy famoso</u> de Costa Rica.
4. La moneda oficial de Costa Rica es el <u>colón</u>.
5. Desde 1948 Costa Rica <u>tiene</u> ejército.

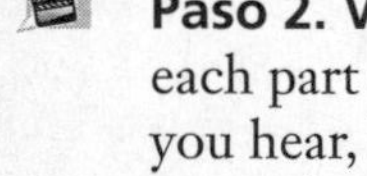

Paso 2. Vistas culturales. View the video segments in order to complete each part of the activity. You will likely not understand all of the words that you hear, but you should relax because you are capable of understanding more than enough to be able to respond to the questions without difficulty. Please be sure to read the questions that you will have to answer before viewing each video segment.

Costa Rica: Introducción. Read the questions, view the video, and then choose the correct response or responses to each question.

6. ¿Con qué país o países tiene Costa Rica frontera (*border*)?
   Panamá
   Colombia
   Nicaragua
   Honduras

7. ¿Con qué masa de agua (*body of water*) o masas de agua tiene costa?
   el Océano Pacífico
   el Mar Caribe

8. ¿En qué año llega Cristóbal Colón a Costa Rica?
   1500 1512
   1502 1520

9. ¿En cuál de sus viajes (*voyages*) a América llega Colón a Costa Rica?
   segundo
   tercero
   cuarto
   quinto

10. ¿Cómo se llaman los costarricenses?
    españoles
    indígenas
    afrocaribeños
    ticos

Nombre: ______________________ Fecha: ______________________

Costa Rica: San José. Read the questions, view the video, and then choose the correct response or responses to each question.

11. ¿Qué puedes hacer en la Plaza de la Cultura de San José?
    ir de compras
    ir a eventos culturales
    dar un paseo

12. ¿Dónde puedes ver arte de la época precolombina?
    la Plaza de la Cultura
    el Museo de Oro
    el Teatro Nacional

13. ¿Dónde hay eventos artísticos nacionales e internacionales?
    la Plaza de la Cultura
    el Museo de Oro
    el Teatro Nacional

Costa Rica: Turismo. Read the questions, view the video, and then choose the correct response or responses to each question.

14. ¿Cuántos turistas visitan Costa Rica cada año?
    200.000
    2.000.000
    20.000.000

15. ¿Qué actividades turísticas puedes practicar en Costa Rica?
    surf
    rafting
    ecoturismo

05-51 Panamá.

Paso 1. Les presento mi país. Read the following statements and, based on the information in your textbook, decide whether or not they convey correct information. Rewrite the selected portions of the incorrect statements in order to make them true. If they are correct, then leave the statement as is.

1. Colón es el nombre de <u>un importante canal</u> y puerto de Panamá.

2. Magdalena vive cerca del <u>Océano Pacífico</u>.

3. <u>El sector de la agricultura</u> es muy importante a la economía de Panamá.

4. <u>Las islas San Blas</u> son un destino turístico importante en Panamá.

5. <u>Kunas</u> son una parte de la ropa tradicional de un grupo de indígenas.

Paso 2. Vistas culturales. View the video segments in order to complete each part of the activity. You will likely not understand all of the words that you hear, but you should relax because you are capable of understanding more than enough to be able to respond to the questions without difficulty. Please be sure to read the questions that you will have to answer before viewing each video segment.

Panamá: Introducción. Read the questions, view the video, and then choose the correct response or responses to each question.

6. ¿Qué población tiene Panamá?
   más de 300.000 habitantes
   más de 3.000.000 de habitantes
   más de 30.000.000 de habitantes

7. ¿Con qué países tiene frontera (*border*)?
   Nicaragua
   Costa Rica
   Venezuela
   Colombia

8. ¿Cuántas costas tiene Panamá?
   una
   dos
   tres

Panamá: Geografía y clima. Read the questions, view the video, and then choose the correct response or responses to each question.

9. ¿Qué tiempo hace en Panamá?
   Hace calor.
   Hace sol.
   Hace frío.
   Nieva mucho.

10. ¿Cuántos kilómetros de costa tiene?
    casi 250
    casi 2.500
    casi 25.000

Panamá: Capital. Read the questions, view the video, and then choose the correct response or responses to each question.

11. ¿Qué hay en la capital de Panamá?
    música
    centros comerciales
    discotecas
    restaurantes

12. ¿Por qué es importante la Zona Libre de Colón?
    Tiene bancos nacionales.
    Es cosmopolita.
    Allí importan y exportan muchos productos.

Nombre: ______________________ Fecha: ______________________

Más cultura

05-52 ¿Quedamos para salir? Read the following information about movie going and other customs related to socializing in the Spanish-speaking world, and then answer the questions.

- En muchos lugares hispanohablantes, es menos frecuente la costumbre estadounidense de quedar con los amigos para ver la televisión o para ver una película en la casa de una persona. Como en muchos lugares anglohablantes, en muchos lugares del mundo hispanohablante es común quedar con los amigos para salir a ver una película o para ir a un concierto o al teatro. Muchos hispanos dicen que "viven en la calle" lo cual demuestra una preferencia por pasar mucho tiempo en espacios públicos.
- Cuando hablan de sus planes, las personas en países hispanohablantes se refieren a "las cuatro de la tarde" o "las diez de la noche"; sin embargo, en la mayoría de los países hispanohablantes, puedes ver muchos horarios oficiales con el sistema de veinticuatro horas. Por ejemplo, en el cine, el horario de proyección de una película normalmente no indica 1:00, 4:30, 6:00 o 7:30, sino 13:00, 16:30, 18:00 y 19:30. 
- Después de un evento como una película, un concierto o una obra en el teatro, en el mundo hispanohablante es muy común ir a tomar algo y para charlar o hablar sobre el evento. Las personas intercambian (*exchange*) sus opiniones y sus ideas sobre las habilidades de los artistas y sobre las ideas que un evento artístico comunica.
- Entre los más jóvenes, la costumbre de "salir por ahí" con todos los amigos es más popular que la costumbre de salir solamente en pareja. Dentro de los grupos de amigos muchas veces hay parejas de novios, pero en vez de salir solos, prefieren salir todos juntos.

1. ¿Por qué crees que muchas personas prefieren ver películas en casa con sus amigos en los Estados Unidos?

____

____

2. ¿Por qué crees que muchas personas prefieren salir a ver películas en el cine con sus amigos en muchos países hispanohablantes?

____

____

3. Usando el sistema de veinticuatro horas, ¿cómo se escribe 1:00 pm, 5:00 pm y 10:00 pm?

____

4. Aparte del mundo hispanohablante, ¿dónde más usan el sistema de veinticuatro horas?

____

____

5. ¿Qué ventajas tiene el uso del sistema de veinticuatro horas? ¿Qué desventajas tiene?

6. ¿Qué piensas de la costumbre de salir después para tomar algo y hablar sobre una película o un concierto? ¿Tienes tú la misma costumbre? ¿Piensas que muchos estadounidenses también hacen eso?

7. ¿Sales más frecuentemente en grupo con todos tus amigos o con solamente una persona? ¿Cuál de las dos opciones prefieres? ¿Por qué?

05-53 Heritage Language: *tu mundo hispano*. Conduct research on the music of a Spanish-speaking country. If you are of Spanish-speaking heritage, choose a musician or group from your family's country of origin. If you are not, then interview a friend, relative, or fellow student who is of Spanish-speaking heritage and research an artist or a band from that person's country of origin.

Paso 1. Use the following questions as a guide for your research and write down notes about the information that you discover.

- ¿Cómo se llama?
- ¿De dónde es?
- ¿Qué tipo(s) de música toca?
- ¿Qué instrumento(s) toca? ¿Cómo lo(s) toca?
- ¿Cómo se llaman sus canciones más famosas?
- ¿Cómo son las canciones? ¿Cómo es la letra de las canciones?
- ¿Dónde da conciertos? ¿Hace giras nacionales? ¿Hace giras internacionales?
- ¿Te gusta su música? ¿Por qué sí o por qué no?

Paso 2. Describe the artist or band that you chose to research and the music that this person or this group has created. As you speak, try to use words like **y, pero,** and **también** to lengthen your sentences and connect your ideas.

Nombre: ______________________________ Fecha: ______________________

Ambiciones siniestras

Episodio 5

Lectura: *La búsqueda de Eduardo*
(Textbook p. 198)

05-54 La búsqueda de Eduardo. Select the correct answer or answers to the following questions about this episode of *Ambiciones siniestras*. For each question, more than one answer may be correct.

1. ¿A quiénes piensa Cisco que debe llamar?
   A los amigos de Eduardo
   A los compañeros de clase
   A la policía
   A los padres de Eduardo

2. ¿Cómo puede entrar Cisco en el correo de Eduardo?
   Sabe la contraseña (*password*).
   Encuentra la contraseña.
   Sabe mucho de computadoras.
   Tiene mucha suerte.

3. ¿Qué tipo de grupo toca esta noche en la universidad de Cisco?
   Un grupo cuyo (*whose*) cantante toca la guitarra muy bien
   Un grupo local que tiene grabaciones fenomenales
   Un grupo que siempre tiene buenos programas de música
   Un grupo muy famoso por todo el mundo

4. ¿Con quién va al concierto Cisco?
   Va solo.
   Va con Eduardo.
   Va con su primo Manolo.
   Va con la chica guapísima de su clase de economía.

5. ¿Por qué no quiere dormir Cisco?
   Está pensando en Eduardo.
   Está pensando en la chica guapísima.
   Está pensando en su primo.
   Está pensando en el concierto.

Video: *Se conocen* (Textbook p. 200)

05-55 Se conocen. View the episode and indicate what information each finalist shares about himself o herself.

1. Cisco — Dónde vive — De dónde es — Dónde estudia — Qué estudia

2. Alejandra — Dónde vive — De dónde es — Dónde estudia — Qué estudia

3. Manolo — Dónde vive — De dónde es — Dónde estudia — Qué estudia

4. Marisol — Dónde vive — De dónde es — Dónde estudia — Qué estudia

5. Lupe — Dónde vive — De dónde es — Dónde estudia — Qué estudia

05-56 ¿Qué pasa en el episodio? View the episode again, and then answer the following questions.

1. ¿Cómo está Marisol cuando el episodio empieza?
   tranquila
   enojada
   contenta
   nerviosa

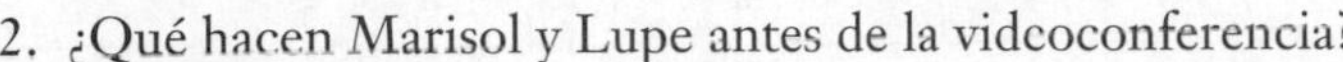

2. ¿Qué hacen Marisol y Lupe antes de la videoconferencia?
   Van de compras.
   Comen.
   Van a clase.
   Terminan un trabajo.

3. ¿Qué hacen Manolo y Alejandra antes de la videoconferencia?
   Van de compras.
   Comen.
   Van a clase.
   Terminan un trabajo.

4. ¿A qué hora empieza la videoconferencia?
   a las 15:00
   a las 16:00
   a las 17:00
   a las 18:00

5. ¿Qué le confiesa Manolo a Alejandra antes de ir a su casa?
   Cisco es su primo.
   Cisco es su amigo.
   Cisco es el novio de su hermana.
   No le gusta Cisco.

6. ¿Qué le dice Manolo a Alejandra sobre Eduardo?
   Eduardo es su primo.
   Eduardo está terminando un trabajo importante.
   Nadie sabe dónde está Eduardo.
   No le gusta Eduardo.

7. ¿Quiénes quieren llamar a la policía?
   Cisco
   Manolo
   Alejandra
   Lupe
   Marisol

05-57 ¿Qué piensas? Read the following questions, view the episode again, and then answer the following questions about this episode and what you imagine is to come in the next episodes.

1. ¿Qué piensas que ocurre con Alejandra? ¿Dónde piensas que está? ¿Con quién(es) crees que está? ¿Por qué crees que desaparece (*disappears*)?

____

____

____

____

2. ¿Qué piensas que va a pasar en los próximos episodios? ¿Qué van a hacer Cisco, Manolo, Marisol y Lupe? ¿Qué va a ocurrir con ellos?

____

____

____

____

Comunidades

05-58 Experiential Learning: El cine y la música. Ask your library to order copies of one of the films listed below (or another film recommended by your instructor) so that you may view it. Once you have seen it, write a brief analysis of the film, honing in on the role and importance of music in it.

Suggested films:

- *Chico y Rita* (Fernando Trueba and Javier Mariscal, 2010)
- *The Lost City* (Andy García, 2005)
- *Viva Cuba* (Juan Carlos Cremata Malberti, 2005)
- *Suite Habana* (Fernando Pérez, 2003)
- *La lengua de las mariposas* (José Luis Cuerda, 1999)
- *Azúcar amarga* (León Ichaso, 1996)

05-59 Service Learning: Un festival de cine. Ask your library to order copies of the films listed below (or films recommended by your instructor) so that you and your classmates may organize a Hispanic film festival on your campus. Conduct research on the films, their director and actors, and their soundtracks. Gear the information towards an audience that is unfamiliar with Hispanic films. Make certain to also prepare a handout with information about the cultural practices that can be observed in the film, especially those that differ from common practices of a non-Hispanic audience. Before the projection of each film during the film festival, you and your classmates should introduce the film by giving a brief presentation of the results of your research.

Films to consider including:

- *La piel que habito* (Pedro Almodóvar, 2011)
- *Biutiful* (Alejandro González Iñárritu, 2011)
- *Alatriste* (Agustín Díaz Yanes, 2006)
- *The Lost City* (Andy García, 2005)
- *Viva Cuba* (Juan Carlos Cremata Malberti, 2005)
- *Suite Habana* (Fernando Pérez, 2003)
- *Nueve reinas* (Fabián Bielinsky, 2000)
- *La lengua de las mariposas* (José Luis Cuerda, 1999)
- *Tesis* (Alejandro Amenábar, 1996)
- *Azúcar amarga* (León Ichaso, 1996)

Nombre: ______________________ Fecha: ______________________

6 ¡Sí, lo sé!

Capítulo Preliminar A, Capítulo 1 y Capítulo 2 (Textbook p. 207)

06-01 Descripciones. Listen to each description, and write the letter of the image that it describes. If both images apply, then write *los dos*.

1. a.  b.  ______________

2. a.  b.  ______________

3. a.  b.  ______________

4. a.  b. 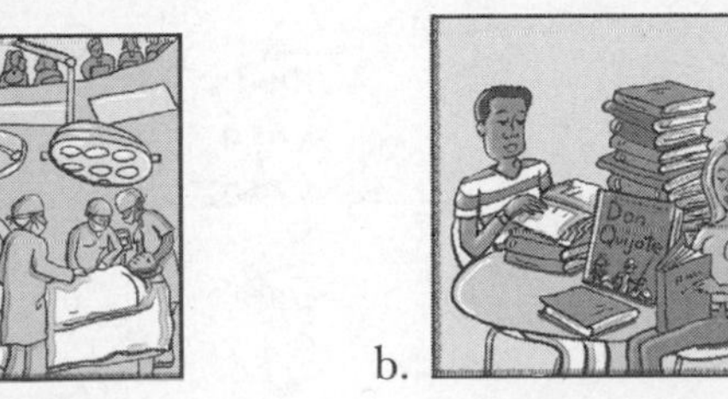

____

5. a.  b.  ______________

Nombre: ______________________ Fecha: ______________________

06-02 La familia de Olga.

Paso 1. Olga is a new friend at your university. She is showing you pictures of her family and describing her siblings to you. Listen to her description, and select all the words you hear.

1. ____ alto ____ inteligente ____ estudioso

____ trabajador ____ interesantes ____ bueno

____ perezoso ____ responsable ____ simpáticos

____ delgadas ____ aburrido ____ guapos

____ cómico ____ pequeños

Paso 2. Now select the family member(s) that each adjective characterizes. If you need to, listen to her description again.

2. trabajador/a
   Olga
   Carlos
   Susana
   Pablo
   Alicia

3. perezoso/a
   Olga
   Carlos
   Susana
   Pablo
   Alicia

4. responsable
   Olga
   Carlos
   Susana
   Pablo
   Alicia

5. irresponsable
   Olga
   Carlos
   Susana
   Pablo
   Alicia

6. inteligente
   Olga
   Carlos
   Susana
   Pablo
   Alicia

7. atlético/a
   Olga
   Carlos
   Susana
   Pablo
   Alicia

8. simpático/a
   Olga
   Carlos
   Susana
   Pablo
   Alicia

9. guapo/a
   Olga
   Carlos
   Susana
   Pablo
   Alicia

10. pequeño/a
    Olga
    Carlos
    Susana
    Pablo
    Alicia

06-03 Las mujeres y los hombres. Your friend is reviewing some notes from his Spanish class in which the teacher described two famous people—Puerto Rican singer and actress, Jennifer López, and Spanish actor, Javier Bardem. Unfortunately, his notes are a mess and it is difficult to tell which adjectives his professor used to describe which person. Look at the descriptions below, and use your knowledge of Spanish grammar to figure out which person(s) they apply to. If the answer is unclear, select **No se sabe**.

1. bonita
   a. Jennifer López
   b. Javier Bardem
   c. Jennifer López y Javier Bardem
   d. No se sabe.

2. morenos
   a. Jennifer López
   b. Javier Bardem
   c. Jennifer López y Javier Bardem
   d. No se sabe.

3. interesante
   a. Jennifer López
   b. Javier Bardem
   c. Jennifer López y Javier Bardem
   d. No se sabe.

4. guapo
   a. Jennifer López
   b. Javier Bardem
   c. Jennifer López y Javier Bardem
   d. No se sabe.

5. tiene mucho talento
   a. Jennifer López
   b. Javier Bardem
   c. Jennifer López y Javier Bardem
   d. No se sabe.

6. español
   a. Jennifer López
   b. Javier Bardem
   c. Jennifer López y Javier Bardem
   d. No se sabe.

7. inteligente
   a. Jennifer López
   b. Javier Bardem
   c. Jennifer López y Javier Bardem
   d. No se sabe.

8. delgados
   a. Jennifer López
   b. Javier Bardem
   c. Jennifer López y Javier Bardem
   d. No se sabe.

9. baja
   a. Jennifer López
   b. Javier Bardem
   c. Jennifer López y Javier Bardem
   d. No se sabe.

10. tienen mucho éxito en Los Estados Unidos y también en otros países
    a. Jennifer López
    b. Javier Bardem
    c. Jennifer López y Javier Bardem
    d. No se sabe.

06-04 ¿Sabes dónde está? Maribel is a new transfer student at school and does not know her way around very well. Listen to her conversation with Adrián, and then select the correct answer to each of the following questions.

1. Maribel está
   a. confundida.
   b. perdida.
   c. dormida.
   d. pedida.

2. Maribel ________________ la Facultad de Ciencias.
   a. busca
   b. sabe dónde está
   c. no ve
   d. le pide ayuda a

3. La Facultad de Ciencias
   a. es pequeña.
   b. es enorme y moderna.
   c. está cerca del Edificio Central.
   d. no tiene mucha luz (*light*) natural.

4. La Facultad de Filosofía
   a. está en la cafetería.
   b. es donde trabaja el tío de Adrián.
   c. está lejos del gimnasio.
   d. no está cerca de la Facultad de Ciencias.

5. La oficina del Profesor Rubio
   a. está en un edificio moderno.
   b. tiene muchas ventanas.
   c. está en el Edificio Central.
   d. es el número 375.

06-05 Heritage Language: *tu español*. Listen to each statement, and then indicate which of the easily confused words the speaker is using.

1. por qué — porque
2. cómo — como
3. está — esta
4. va a ser — va a hacer
5. está siendo — está haciendo

Nombre: ______________________ Fecha: ______________________

Capítulo 3 (Textbook p. 210)

06-06 ¿Dónde están? For each statement about what the family member is doing, select the location in the house that most logically corresponds.

1. Mi hermana está preparando la comida en...
   a. la cocina
   b. el altillo
   c. el jardín
   d. la oficina

2. Mi padre está organizando sus papeles en...
   a. el garaje
   b. la cocina
   c. el baño
   d. la oficina

3. Mi hermano está trabajando en su automóvil en...
   a. el garaje
   b. la cocina
   c. el jardín
   d. la oficina

4. Mi madre tiene una conversación por teléfono muy importante y muy privada con mi tía en...
   a. el garaje
   b. el jardín
   c. el dormitorio
   d. la cocina

5. Voy a salir esta noche a un restaurante romántico con mi novio; me estoy preparando en...
   a. el sótano
   b. la cocina
   c. el jardín
   d. el baño

6. Mi hermano está buscando fotos antiguas y otros recuerdos (*mementos*) de la familia en...
   a. la cocina
   b. el altillo
   c. el jardín
   d. el baño

Nombre: ______________________ Fecha: ______________________

06-07 Una casa interesante. Your friend is working part-time at a real estate agency. Just as you stop by to visit, she receives a phone call from one of the agent's clients. Look below at the answers that she gives, and write the question that the client asked. Follow the model closely.

MODELO *¿Cuántos dormitorios tiene?*
Tiene cuatro dormitorios.

1. ¿______________________?

   Tiene dos baños.

2. ¿______________________?

   No, no tiene sótano.

3. ¿______________________?

   Sí, tiene un altillo muy grande.

4. ¿______________________?

   Sí, tiene un jardín grande.

5. ¿______________________?

   Cuesta cuatrocientos setenta y cinco mil dólares.

6. ¿______________________?

   Está en el centro del pueblo.

06-08 Los famosos. You are the guest host of *Lifestyles of the Rich and Famous*. You are preparing to interview a famous person who you find particularly intriguing and interesting. First, choose the person that you would like to interview, and then list at least six questions that you will ask the person about his or her home and lifestyle in general.

Persona famosa: ______________________

1. ______________________
2. ______________________
3. ______________________
4. ______________________
5. ______________________
6. ______________________

Nombre: ______________________ Fecha: ______________________

06-09 Entrevista con un posible empleado. You are a famous and extremely wealthy person living in a very large house. Because you are so busy and successful and your house is so large, you do not have time to attend to all of the household chores. You need to hire someone to help you as a live-in domestic employee.

Paso 1. Write down notes about what kinds of tasks you will need the person to take care of and what kind of traits you are looking for in your new employee.

1. Quehaceres y responsabilidades:

____

____

____

2. Características importantes:

____

____

____

Paso 2. A potential employee has responded to your ad and would like more information about the position. You have returned the call, but the person is not home. Leave a message giving as much detail as possible as to the kind of person you would like to hire, the types of responsibilities the person would have if hired, and what kind of pay and living arrangements you are prepared to offer.

06-10 Heritage Language: *tu español*. Practice spelling words containing letters that are easily confused. Write each statement that you hear.

1. ______________________
2. ______________________
3. ______________________
4. ______________________

Capítulo 4 (Textbook p. 213)

06-11 Por la ciudad. Associate each place with the activities that people normally do there.

1. correos ______
2. el supermercado ______
3. la plaza ______
4. el cine ______
5. la iglesia ______
6. el cajero automático ______
7. el museo ______
8. la discoteca ______
9. el almacén ______
10. el restaurante ______

a. Bailamos toda la noche.
b. Compro comida para cocinar.
c. Saca dinero para comprar cosas.
d. Estudiamos obras de arte.
e. Ven películas.
f. Practican su religión.
g. Almuerzan con los amigos.
h. Compran ropa y otras cosas para su familia.
i. Camino y hablo con mis amigos.
j. Mando cartas a mis amigos.

Nombre: ______________________________ Fecha: ______________________

06-12 El horario de Fabio. Look at the following excerpt from Fabio's schedule for next week, and then answer the questions using complete sentences.

MODELO ¿Qué va a hacer a las once el domingo?
A las once, *va a jugar al fútbol.*

	lunes	**martes**	**miércoles**	**jueves**	**viernes**	**sábado**	**domingo**
8:00	tomar café	dormir	tomar café	dormir	tomar café	dormir	dormir
9:00	clase de economía	tomar café	clase de economía	tomar café	clase de economía	dormir	dormir
9:30		trabajar		trabajar		tomar café	tomar café
10:00	clase de biología		clase de biología		clase de biología	estudiar en la biblioteca	jugar al fútbol
11:00	clase de literatura		clase de literatura		clase de literatura		
12:00	almorzar		almorzar		almorzar		
13:00	hacer la tarea	almorzar	hacer la tarea	almorzar	hacer la tarea	almorzar	almorzar con los amigos
14:00	clase de español	clase de arte	clase de español	clase de arte	clase de español	estudiar en la biblioteca	
15:00	trabajar		trabajar		trabajar	hacer ejercicio en el gimnasio	descansar
15:30		hacer la tarea y estudiar		hacer la tarea y estudiar			

1. ¿Qué va a hacer el domingo a las nueve y media?

   El domingo a las nueve y media, ______________________.

2. ¿Qué va a hacer el martes a las diez y cuarto?

   El martes a las diez y cuarto, ______________________.

3. ¿Qué va a hacer el sábado a las ocho de la mañana?

   El sábado a las ocho, ______________________.

4. ¿Qué va a hacer el viernes a la una y cuarto?

   El viernes a la una y cuarto, ______________________.

5. ¿Qué va a hacer el lunes a las tres y media?

   El lunes a las tres y media, ______________________.

6. ¿Qué va a hacer el sábado a las tres y cuarto?

   El sábado a las tres y cuarto, ______________________.

06-13 ¿Cómo puedes servir a tu comunidad? Listen to each statement about peoples' different talents and abilities, and then choose the best way for each person to serve their community.

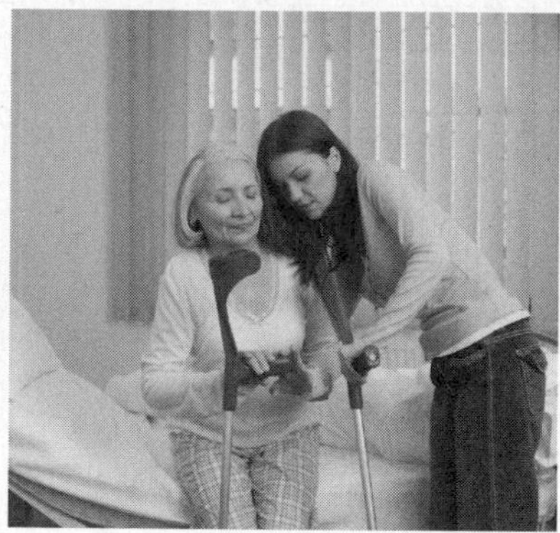

1. ______ a. Puedes circular una petición.
2. ______ b. Puedes dar un concierto y dar el dinero a la comunidad.
3. ______ c. Puedes visitar a los ancianos en una residencia.
4. ______ d. Puedes dar clases de artesanía.
5. ______ e. Puedes hablar a favor de una causa importante en tu comunidad.
6. ______ f. Puedes trabajar en un campamento de niños.

Nombre: ______________________ Fecha: ______________________

06-14 Tu comunidad. Prepare to describe some of the challenges that your community faces and some of the ways that you can help your community face those challenges.

Paso 1. Answer **sí** or **no** to the following survey questions about your community.

1. ¿Hay problemas de crimen? ______________
2. ¿Hay problemas de violencia? ______________
3. ¿Hay problemas con las drogas ilegales? ______________
4. ¿Hay una división grande entre los ricos y los pobres? ______________
5. ¿Hay personas sin (que no tienen) casa en tu comunidad? ______________
6. ¿Hay personas que tienen hambre? ______________
7. ¿Tienen todos los niños acceso a buenos tutores para ayudarles con su tarea? ______________
8. ¿Hay muchas personas en tu comunidad que necesitan ayuda? ______________
9. ¿Hay muchas organizaciones sin fines de lucro (*non-profit*) en tu comunidad? ______________
10. ¿Te gusta la idea de ayudar a un grupo de personas o a una organización? ______________

Paso 2. Write a description of your community and the current challenges it faces. Then describe what people in your community currently do to serve others, and what you plan to do in the future in order to contribute as well. Write a minimum of ten sentences.

____

____

____

____

____

____

____

____

____

____

06-15 Cómo servimos a nuestra comunidad. Talk about your community, and how you and other community members work to serve and create a better environment for everyone. Try to speak for at least 2 minutes.

Capítulo 5 (Textbook p. 216)

06-16 Música. Listen to each statement, and then identify which statement describes each image.

1. ______

2. ______

3. ______

4. ______

5. ______

a. Statement A

b. Statement B

c. Statement C

d. Statement D

e. Statement E

Nombre: ______________________ Fecha: ______________________

06-17 Cine. Listen to each statement, and then identify which statement describes each image.

1. ______ 

2. ______ 

3. ______ 

4. ______ 

5. ______

a. Statement A

b. Statement B

c. Statement C

d. Statement D

e. Statement E

Nombre: ______________________ Fecha: ______________________

06-18 Música y cine. Complete the following crossword puzzle.

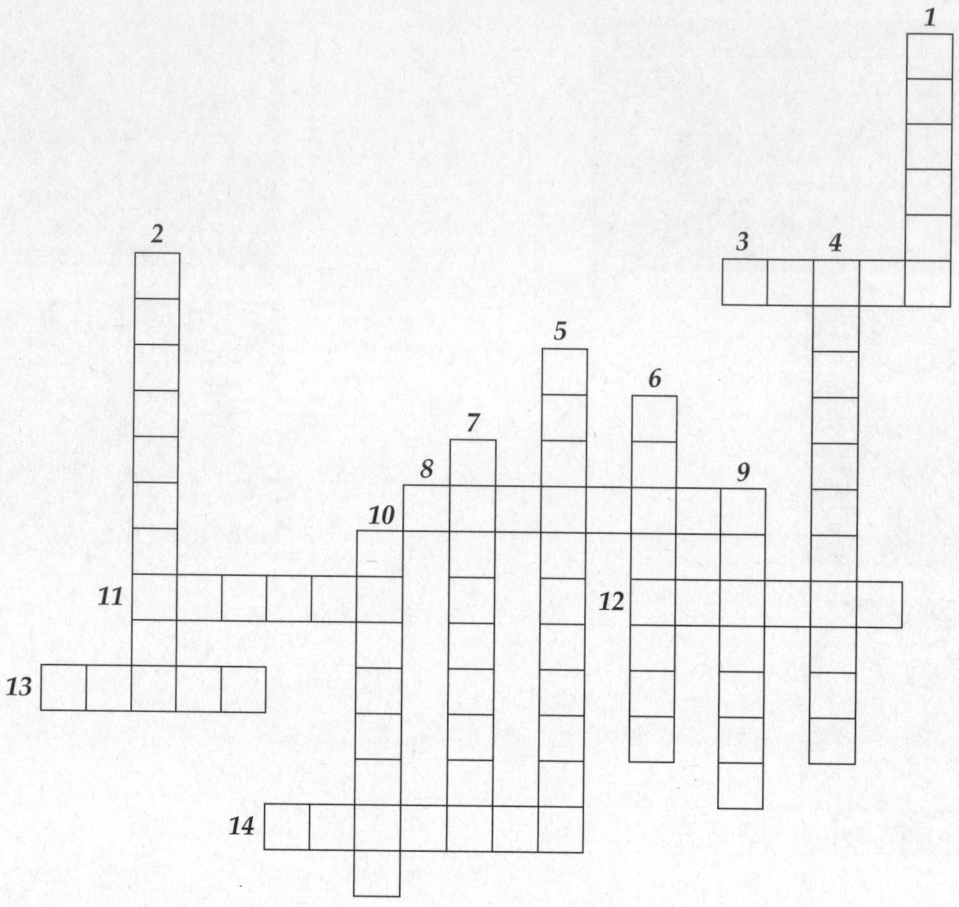

1. *Saving Private Ryan* es una película de ________________.
2. Un género de película que no es ficción es una película ________________.
3. Las palabras de una canción son la ________________.
4. Arturo Sandoval es un ________________ del jazz latino muy importante.
5. Eric Clapton es un ________________ de rock muy famoso.
6. La cosa en el cine sobre la que (*on which*) proyectan las películas es la ________________.
7. Un músico de rock que toca un instrumento de percusión es el ________________.
8. Un músico que canta las canciones es el ________________.
9. El primer día que se proyecta una película en el cine, es el día del ________________.
10. Para dar un concierto de música clásica, es necesario tener una ________________ de músicos.
11. Un instrumento de percusión que usan frecuentemente en el jazz latino es el ________________.
12. La protagonista de una película es una ________________.
13. Un género muy popular y también muy importante de la música caribeña es la ________________.
14. La cosa que tienes que comprar para entrar en el cine es una ________________.

Nombre: ______________________ Fecha: ______________________

06-19 Un concierto en la Concha Acústica. Imagine that you are studying abroad in Managua, Nicaragua, and that one of your favorite bands is giving a concert in **la Concha Acústica**. Imagine that you are at the concert. Look at the picture below, and describe the Managua Lake, the concert, the music, and what is going on around you in general.

____

____

____

____

____

____

____

____

____

06-20 Heritage Language: *tu español*. Match each instrument to the country with which it is most closely associated.

1. txistu ______	a. Panamá
2. quijongo ______	b. Costa Rica
3. cajón ______	c. Perú
4. mejoranera ______	d. Ecuador
5. rondador ______	e. España

Un poco de todo (Textbook p. 218)

06-21 Las descripciones. Your friend from Spanish class is having difficulty recalling the meaning of all of the adjectives that you have learned throughout this course. Help out by selecting the word in each group that refers to a negative or unfavorable characteristic.

1. guapo	aburrido	divertido	interesante
2. simpática	inteligente	pésima	generosa
3. bueno	cómico	antipático	bonito
4. malo	hábil	estupendo	sorprendente
5. impresionante	creativa	joven	perezoso
6. graciosa	importante	irresponsable	creativa

Nombre: ______________________ Fecha: ______________________

06-22 Ayuda para una amiga.

Paso 1. Tablas incompletas. Your friend from Spanish class is having difficulty recalling all of the different verb forms. Help out by completing the verb charts.

ser			
singular		plural	
yo	(1)	nosotros	(3)
tú	(2)	vosotros	sois
él, ella, usted	es	ellos, ellas, ustedes	son
tener			
singular		plural	
yo	(4)	nosotros	(6)
tú	tienes	vosotros	tenéis
él, ella, usted	(5)	ellos, ellas, ustedes	(7)
gustar			
singular		plural	
a mí	(8)	a nosotros	(9)
a ti	te gusta/n	a vosotros	os gusta/n
a él, ella, usted	le gusta/n	a ellos, ellas, ustedes	(10)

Paso 2. Las formas de los verbos. Your friend would also like to try a different approach to reviewing the different verb forms. She created a list of verbs and forms that she wants to use to talk about herself and her family. Help her by completing the lists of forms.

	yo	nosotros	él / ella	ellos / ellas
11. ser				
12. estar				
13. tener				
14. gustar				
15. querer				
16. empezar				
17. pedir				
18. poder				
19. almorzar				
20. vivir				

Nombre: ______________________________ Fecha: ______________________

06-23 Unas vacaciones. Listen as Sofía and her friends discuss their vacation plans, and then complete the statements about their preferences, as in the model.

MODELO África quiere visitar otro lugar durante las vacaciones porque donde ella vive *hace mucho frío*.

1. Sofía quiere ir a ______________ o ______________
2. Sofía está estudiando dos países centroamericanos en su clase de ______________ hispánicas.
3. África piensa que en Honduras pueden ______________ por la playa, ______________ el sol y ______________ acuáticos.
4. Mario cree que pueden ______________ los bosques del país.
5. Sofía quiere ______________ las ruinas de Copán y ______________ sobre las ______________ indígenas.
6. Mañana Mario va a ______________ en Internet para ______________ los precios para el viaje.
7. Esta tarde Sofía va a ______________ a la ______________ para ______________ una guía turística.
8. Ahora África va a ______________ a su amiga para ______________ ayuda.

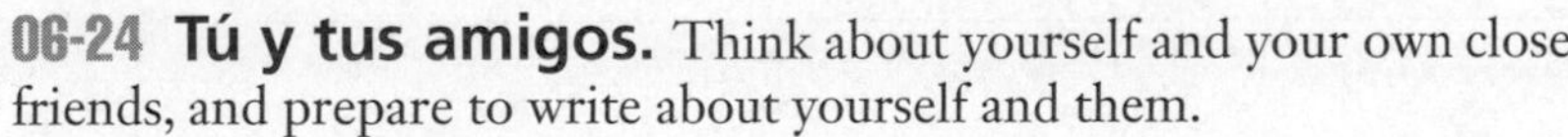

06-24 Tú y tus amigos. Think about yourself and your own close friends, and prepare to write about yourself and them.

Paso 1. Using the following questions as a guide, jot down as many notes as possible with basic information about yourself and about your three friends that will help you as you create your description.

- ¿Cómo es físicamente?
- ¿Cómo es su personalidad?
- ¿Cuáles son las cualidades que te gustan mucho de la persona?
- ¿Cuántos años tiene?
- ¿Dónde estudia?
- ¿En qué año de sus estudios está (primero, etc.)?
- ¿Qué estudia?
- ¿Qué le gusta hacer cuando tiene tiempo libre?
- ¿Qué va a hacer durante las vacaciones?

Nombre: ______________________ Fecha: ______________________

1. Yo

2. Amigo/a 1

3. Amigo/a 2

4. Amigo/a 3

Paso 2. Now use the information above and the expressions below to write a description of yourself and your friends, your favorite pastimes, and your vacation plans. Write at least fifteen sentences.

y	*and*	primero	*first*
también	*also*	entonces	*then*
pero	*but*	después	*after*
tampoco	*neither*	luego	*later on*
en contraste	*in contrast*		

Nombre: ______________________________ Fecha: ______________________

06-25 Mis amigos y yo. Talk about yourself and your friends, your physical characteristics and personality traits, your pastimes, and interests. Try to give your description fluidly and naturally, and to speak for two minutes.

06-26 La librería. Marta and Javier are in the bookstore looking for school supplies. Listen to their conversation with the salesperson, and then answer the following questions using complete sentences. In your answers, use direct object pronouns to replace the direct objects.

MODELO ¿Tienen el libro de matemáticas en la librería?
Sí, lo tienen.
OR
No, no lo tienen.

1. ¿Tienen bolígrafos de color verde en la librería?

____.

2. ¿Quieren comprar Marta y Javier unos lápices?

____.

3. ¿Quién necesita una mochila?

____.

4. ¿Quién ve al Dr. Ibáñez?

____.

5. ¿Van a comer Marta y Javier hamburguesas antes de su clase?

____.

6. ¿Tienen Marta y Javier la clase de literatura hoy?

____.

06-27 El consejero. Maribel and her advisor, Profesor Rubio, are talking about her requirements and study plan. Complete the following statements using the information that you hear and the expressions **tener que** and **hay que**. Be sure to use **tener que** when referring to what one specific individual must do, and **hay que** when referring to rules in general without specifying a particular person.

1. Maribel ______________ tomar ______________ créditos en esta universidad.
2. En la universidad ______________ tomar ______________ clases de idiomas.
3. En la universidad ______________ tomar ______________ clases de ciencias.
4. Después de este año, Maribel ______________ tomar ______________ clase de ciencias.
5. Para hacer la especialidad de filosofía, ______________ tomar ______________ créditos.
6. El semestre que viene, Maribel ______________ tomar la clase de filosofía ______________.

06-28 Ayuda con los verbos. Your friend from Spanish class is preparing a paragraph about himself and his life at school, but is unsure about how to accurately use different verb forms.

Paso 1. Review his notes and select the words that are verbs.

1. ser un estudiante, universidad muy grande.
2. tener muchas clases muy interesantes, gustar mucho
3. conocer a muchas personas, saber todos sus nombres
4. todos los días: jugar al fútbol, yo preferir el fútbol americano, pero mis amigos tener otras preferencias.
5. fines de semana: salir con mis amigos, este fin de semana ir a bailar en una fiesta

Paso 2. Now help your friend by writing the correct verb forms to complete his description.

Yo (6) ser un estudiante en una universidad muy grande. (7) Tener muchas clases muy interesantes, (8) gustar mucho mis clases. (9) Conocer a muchas personas en mis clases y (10) saber todos sus nombres. Mis amigos y yo (11) jugar al fútbol todos los días. Yo (12) preferir el fútbol americano, pero mis amigos (13) tener otras preferencias. Los fines de semana yo siempre (14) salir con mis amigos. Este fin de semana (15) ir a bailar mucho en una fiesta.

Nombre: ________________________ Fecha: ____________________

06-29 Tu vida en la universidad. Prepare to give a description of yourself and your life at school.

Paso 1. Jot down your responses to the following questions in order to trigger as many ideas as possible.

1. ¿Es este tu primer año? ¿el segundo? ¿el tercero?

   ____

2. ¿Cuántas clases tomas? ¿Qué clases tomas?

   ____

3. ¿Cuáles son tus clases favoritas? ¿Por qué te gustan?

   ____

4. ¿Cuáles son las clases que no te gustan? ¿Por qué no te gustan?

   ____

5. ¿Dónde vives? ¿en una casa? ¿un apartamento? ¿una residencia?

   ____

6. ¿Vives solo/a o con otra(s) persona(s)? ¿Por qué? Si tienes compañero(s) de cuarto o de casa, ¿te gusta(n) esta(s) persona(s)? ¿Por qué sí o por qué no?

   ____

7. ¿Te gusta el lugar donde vives? ¿Por qué sí o por qué no?

   ____

8. ¿Conoces a muchas personas en tu universidad? ¿Cómo son?

   ____

9. ¿Trabajas? Si sí, ¿dónde? ¿cuántas horas a la semana? ¿Te gusta tu trabajo? ¿Por qué sí o por qué no?

   ____

10. ¿Haces ejercicio frecuentemente? ¿Por qué sí o por qué no? Si haces ejercicio, ¿qué ejercicio haces? ¿dónde? ¿cuándo?

    ____

11. ¿Qué te gusta hacer cuando tienes tiempo libre?

    ____

12. ¿Qué otros aspectos de tu vida en la universidad son muy importantes para ti?

    ____

Paso 2. Now, using your notes from **Paso 1**, write a thorough description of your life at the university. You should write at least fifteen sentences in a cohesive paragraph.

____

____

____

____

____

____

____

____

____

____

____

____

____

____

____

06-30 Give an oral description of your life at the university. You should speak for up to 2 minutes about yourself, your classes and professors, your responsibilities, your friends, and what you do during your free time.

Nombre: ______________________ Fecha: ______________________

06-31 Geografía. Complete the charts with basic information about each country you have studied so far.

Paso 1.

	México	España	Honduras	Guatemala
región del mundo	Norteamérica	(1) ________	(2) ________	Centroamérica
país(es) con los que tiene frontera	Belice, (3) ________ y Estados Unidos	Andorra, (4) ________ y Francia	Guatemala, (5) ________ y Nicaragua	(6) ________, Belice, Honduras y El Salvador
costa(s)	El Océano Pacífico y el Mar Caribe	El Mar Cantábrico, el (7) ________ y el Mar Mediterráneo	El Océano Pacífico y el (8) ________	El Mar Caribe y el (9) ________
capital	(10) ________	Madrid	(11) ________	(12) ________

Paso 2.

	El Salvador	Nicaragua	Costa Rica	Panamá
región del mundo	Centroamérica	Centroamérica	Centroamérica	Centroamérica
país(es) con los que tiene frontera	Honduras y (13) ________	Honduras y (14) ________	Nicaragua y (15) ________	(16) ________ y Colombia
costa(s)	El (17) ________	El (18) ________ y el Mar Caribe	El Océano Pacífico y el (19) ________	El (20) ________ y el Mar Caribe
capital	(21) ________	(22) ________	(23) ________	(24) ________

Nombre: ______________________ Fecha: ______________________

06-32 Culturas de los países hispanohablantes. Based on what you have learned about the cultures of Spanish-speaking countries, indicate if the following statements are **Cierto** or **Falso**.

1. En los países hispanohablantes muchas personas, especialmente las mujeres, se saludan con un besito. Cierto Falso
2. Con personas hispanohablantes, hay que usar la forma "usted" para hablar con los mayores que uno no conoce. Cierto Falso
3. En el mundo hispanohablante, un niño tiene dos apellidos, el primero de su madre y el segundo de su padre. Cierto Falso
4. En muchos países hispanohablantes, el deporte nacional es el fútbol. Cierto Falso
5. St. Augustine, fundada por los españoles, es la primera ciudad europea en los Estados Unidos. Cierto Falso
6. En muchos lugares del mundo hispanohablante no existe el mismo espíritu del voluntariado que en Estados Unidos; las personas que necesitan ayuda tienen que buscarla en organizaciones internacionales. Cierto Falso
7. En la antigüedad, los mayas usaban (*used*) granos de cacao como dinero. Cierto Falso
8. Los Kunas son famosos productos de artesanía de los indígenas de Nicaragua. Cierto Falso
9. Como en muchos otros géneros de música, la música latina está evolucionando; ahora existen muchos nuevos géneros que son el resultado de esa evolución. Cierto Falso
10. Antes de los años 80, no hay actores hispanos importantes en el cine de este país. Cierto Falso

Nombre: ______________________ Fecha: ______________________

06-33 Una visita al mundo hispanohablante. Read the following scenario, and then write a description of your dream trip to a Spanish-speaking country, using a minimum of 12 sentences.

Tienes la oportunidad de hacer un viaje (*trip*) por México y Centroamérica, pero puedes visitar solamente tres países. ¿Qué países vas a visitar? ¿Por qué vas a visitarlos? ¿Qué vas a hacer en cada país, si el dinero no importa?

____

____

____

____

____

____

____

____

____

____

____

____

____

____

06-34 Heritage Language: *tu mundo hispano.* If you are of Spanish-speaking heritage, conduct research on an important person from your family's country of origin whose work relates to the worlds of architecture, social or political activism, film, or television. If you are not of Spanish-speaking heritage, then focus on an important person in one of these areas from one of the Hispanic countries that you have studied so far. Conduct research on the person in order to prepare a podcast for your classmates. You should research:

- the person's family,
- the city or town where she or he is from,
- the city or town where he or she lives currently,
- important highlights of the person's career,
- characteristics of the work that the person does, and
- any other important information that will help your classmates understand the importance of this figure in that country and in the Spanish-speaking world in general.

Your podcast should last 3-5 minutes.

06-35 Experiential Learning: En el cine. Search online for the website of a movie theater somewhere in a Spanish-speaking country. Examine the films that are currently showing, and compare them to the films that your local theater is currently showing.

- How many films are from Spanish-speaking countries?
- How many are from the United States?
- How many are from other countries?
- How many films are in a foreign language?
- In the case of foreign language films, are the film titles translated into Spanish or do they appear in the original?
- Why do you think each place offers the films that they offer?
- What do the results of your research say about each culture and the perspectives of people in each city or town?

Write a brief analytical reflection comparing and contrasting the type, number, and variety of films shown in each place.

06-36 Service Learning: Español para niños. Buy a copy of the Spanish version of Eric Carle's book *Brown Bear, Brown Bear* (*Oso pardo, oso pardo*) in order to donate it to a local Head Start program or preschool.

- Volunteer to read the book to the children and to teach them the colors in Spanish as well as the names of the animals and other vocabulary words that appear in the book.
- Get plenty of practice reading the book before going to the school, so that you can be certain to read the story with correct pronunciation, at an appropriate pace, smoothly and with lively intonation that will engage the children.
- Prepare a podcast of your personal best reading of the story and offer that as an additional gift to the preschool program so that the teachers may create a listening station for the children to return to after you complete your work with them.

Notas

Notas

Notas

Notas

Notas

Notas